BOOKS BY DR. JAMES E. COUNSILMAN

The Complete Book of Swimming (1977)

The Science of Swimming (1968)

The Complete Book of Swimming

The Complete Book

NEW YORK 1977 ATHENEUM

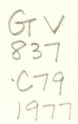
# of Swimming

DR. JAMES E. COUNSILMAN

Swimming Coach and Professor of
Physical Education, Indiana University

Library of Congress Cataloging in Publication Data
Counsilman, James E.
    The complete book of swimming.
    1. Swimming.   I. Title.
GV837.C79   1977   797.2'1   72–82682
ISBN 0–689–10530–4

Published simultaneously in Canada by McClelland and Stewart Ltd.
Composition by Connecticut Printers, Inc., Hartford, Connecticut
Printed and bound by The Murray Printing Company, Forge Village, Massachusetts

Parts of this book appeared in The Science of Swimming and are
reprinted here by permission of Prentice-Hall, Inc.
Drawings by Nora Sheehan
Designed by Kathleen Carey
First Edition

Introduction

YOU MAY THINK I am a little prejudiced, but I feel that swimming is the best form of physical activity there is. I didn't always feel that way. In fact, when I was seven, I almost drowned. It was then I developed a fear of the water that kept me away from it until I was twelve years old. At that time my brother and I went wading in a fish-hatchery pond in Forest Park at St. Louis, Missouri. I stepped into a hole and almost drowned again. After that I decided I had better learn to swim, but I thought maybe I should do it in the safety of a supervised pool—and in shallow water. This is still good advice for all beginners to follow.

I finally did learn to swim when I was thirteen. When I was fourteen, I went out for the high school swimming team and I have been hooked on swimming ever since. I swam competitively until I was twenty-eight years old and in 1970, at the age of forty-nine, when the Masters swimming program started, I made my comeback and am now swimming competitively in the "old folks" swim program. Recently I swam a 1650-yard race in 21:48, which isn't bad for a person who is now in the fifty-five to fifty-nine age division.

In college, when I had to choose a career, I didn't hesitate in deciding that the best possible job for me would be teaching and coaching what I consider to be the best sport of them all—swimming.

Have you wondered why I started this book with an account of my personal experiences? I did so because I want you to understand why there are so many of us swimming nuts in this country. Every sport has a certain number of people who are deeply involved with it and it's no different with swimming. The last time I heard the figure quoted, a half million people were registered in amateur swimming and diving competition. This means that there are also many parents, former swimmers, and just plain interested people who are "swimming nuts" to the point that they spend their free time going to meets or helping run them.

The sport of swimming has been very good to me and I am certain it can provide many pleasant hours for anyone who engages in it. As I sat in the stands at the last Olympic Games, surrounded by a stadiumful of fellow swimming nuts, I realized why we were seeing the American flag and hearing "The Star-Spangled Banner" so often. It was because of these half million kids who had learned to swim at an early age and had gone on to use their skills in competition—the very talented swimmers who had worked hard had continued to improve until they felt they were ready to try for a place on the United States Olympic team.

Perhaps some of you who learn to swim by reading this book and following its suggestions will go on to swim competitively. I'm pretty sure you can already tell that I hope you will. But, even if you don't, you will always have a skill to be proud of.

Everyone should learn to swim. Not just be able to struggle across one width of the pool, but to swim well. There are several obvious reasons why.

1. *Safety*. Over 7000 people drown every year in the United States. Most of these drownings could have been prevented if the victims had only taken the time and made the effort to learn to swim properly.

2. *Physical Fitness and Health*. Experts on fitness agree that swimming is one of the best, if not *the* best, form of exercise. When you swim you use most of the big muscle groups in your body, yet swimming doesn't place undue strain on your joints. Notice that I included the word ''health'' in the heading of this paragraph. That is because swimming is a good exercise for the heart muscle as well as for the skeletal muscles.

3. *Recreation*. Some of the happiest hours you will spend as a child, and even as an adult, will be the time you spend with your friends and family in a pool.

4. *Satisfaction in Mastering a Skill*. As you improve your aquatic skills, you will find that the pleasure that comes from performing efficiently in the water will grow. Of course, this is true of any skill you acquire, but swimming has one unique satisfaction that I have heard many swimmers express. They speak of the good feeling of the water flowing around their body and how, as they become better swimmers, this feeling of flow increases.

5. *Competition*. Many people of nearly all ages now compete in races in the age-group swimming program, in high school, in college, or in the Masters swimming program, where there are even races for people seventy-five years and older.

However, the first goal of this book is to teach you to swim better and to improve your health as well as your skills.

Swimming has done so much for me that I want to repay some of my debt to this sport. If I can help other people share in this enjoyment, that will be a fitting contribution.

This book is for swimmers of every level, from beginning through competitive. The skilled swimmer should skip the first chapter unless he wants to use it as a guide in teaching someone else to swim. Some readers may find it helpful to reread certain chapters several times in order to get a clear idea of exactly what I am trying to say. The chapters that describe each stroke will be among those that need extra attention. Study the pictures and drawings carefully; note particularly the arm pull pattern of each stroke, the amount of bend in the elbow, the position of the body in the water, and so on. It is important to learn correctly the first time and not have to unlearn bad habits later on.

Challenge yourself! Remember that the drills I recommend were not put there just to take up space. Each drill has a specific goal, which is to teach you a necessary skill and help you perfect it. There is also an important progression factor. Skills are usually best learned when they are taught in a certain sequence, progressing from the simple to the more complex.

Another thing I would like to suggest is that you take the book to the pool with you. When you can't remember what to do next, refer to the book.

You can't see yourself performing in the water, so have someone else watch you. Ask the person to read the book and look at the drawings and pictures, then have him tell you how your technique is different from that recommended in the book.

Never feel you have mastered completely all the strokes or skills, but continue to try to improve your technique by practicing with the book nearby to check your progress. Not even Mark Spitz, winner of seven Olympic gold medals (and one of my swimmers here at Indiana

University), felt he could afford to neglect working on technique. On the morning of the day he won his sixth and seventh gold medals, he spent time working on his breathing technique and his flip turn. What I mean is that you should not get complacent when you feel you have become an accomplished swimmer. Part of the fun is to keep trying to get better.

I'm anxious to get started, so let's go.

Contents

The Complete Book
of Swimming

1. The Basic Elements of Good Stroke Mechanics

IT IS IMPORTANT to know not only how to swim correctly, but why you should swim in a certain way. If you understand the physical laws which underlie good stroke mechanics, you can apply them to all your strokes and learn faster and better.

STREAMLINING

Most of these mechanical laws are simple and involve little or no background in fluid mechanics to understand. Take the mechanical principle of streamlining: for a swimmer to progress through the water efficiently he should create as little resistance as possible. His body should present as little surface area to forward progress as possible. That is, he should be in a flat or horizontal position. If the crawl swimmer lifts his head too high, it will cause his legs to drop in the water and he will progress through the water at an angle instead of flat. If his hips or legs wiggle back and forth sideways, he will destroy his efficient streamlining and create additional resistance. This principle applies to all swimming strokes. When you are swimming, you should remain aware of your body position in the water; both the nearness of your feet and legs to the surface of the water and the sideways movement of your body (particularly your hips and legs) should be of concern to you.

BUOYANCY

Most people with their lungs partially inflated are slightly buoyant. That is, they are lighter than water and will float just at the surface with very little of their body out of the water. With this knowledge it is easy to see why the swimmer should not try to elevate himself and swim on top of the water. He is not like a duck, who swims on top of the water; he is more like a dog, who swims with only a small part of himself out of the water. As he goes faster, his body, even though it is almost the same weight as the water, elevates or rises slightly due to the resistance it encounters on the bottom side. This "planing" effect should only be achieved by going faster through creating more propulsion and consequently more forward speed; it should not be achieved by arching the back or by trying to climb on top of the water, as many beginning swimmers and even many advanced competitive swimmers try to do.

ACTION-REACTION LAW

The study of all mechanics is based on Sir Isaac Newton's Three Laws

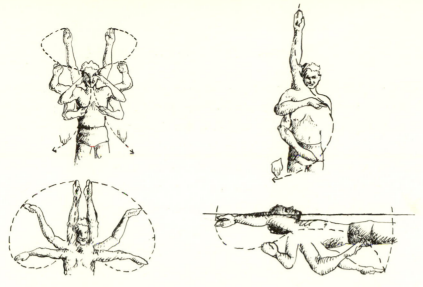

FIG. I   *The Elliptical Pull Pattern of the Four Competitive Strokes*
   a. Butterfly
   b. Crawl stroke
   c. Breaststroke
   d. Backstroke

of Motion. His Third Law states that for every action there is an equal
and opposite reaction. In applying this law to swimming it becomes
clear that for the swimmer to move forward through the water, he must
in some manner push the water backward. However, he should never
push directly backward in a straight line, even though this might ap-
pear to be the most economical method of propulsion. Why shouldn't
he, if he accepts Newton's Third Law? The swimmer *cannot* push the
water directly backward with his feet when kicking the flutter kick, but
the movement of his feet does have a forward-thrust effect. In the
breaststroke kick he can *probably* thrust his feet directly backward in a
straight line, but he does not. Rather, he spreads his feet and then
pushes them backward and together in a diagonally backward direction. The same principle of never pushing directly backward in a
straight line also applies to the arm pull. In all strokes good swimmers
use some variation of an arm pull that follows a single or double

elliptical pattern. Thus, there is a variation of the action-reaction principle involved, which accounts for the fact that pushing the water
directly backward in a straight line is not desirable.

EXPLANATION OF THE ELLIPTICAL PULL PATTERN

Before proceeding with the explanation, let me show you some
examples of the elliptical pull patterns created by good swimmers.
These illustrations will help you understand what I am talking about.

At the end of his leg thrust a runner pushes the ground almost
directly backward. As a result, he is pushed almost directly forward. If
this is true with the runner, should it not also be true of a swimmer in
water? You can immediately recognize the big difference: the runner
pushes against the ground with his feet, the ground remains stationary
and the runner moves forward. If the swimmer pushes directly back
against the water with his feet or hands, the water also moves backward. If he continues to push backward in a straight line, he is pushing
against water that is already moving backward. If the water and his
hands are moving backward at the same speed, the swimmer is no
longer pushing against the water and consequently is receiving no
additional forward thrust. To solve the problem he must move his
hands in an elliptical pattern in order to be constantly getting away
from the water that he has started backward and to encounter water that
is stationary. Another way of stating this principle is this: maximum
efficiency for propulsion in water is achieved by moving a lot of water
a short distance versus moving a little water a great distance.

Before we understood this important principle, swimming instruc-
tors and coaches often spoke of the swimmer grabbing a handful of
water and, keeping that same handful of water, pushing it straight
back. Now we know this is exactly what we don't want him to do.
Exactly how much zigzag (elliptical) movement of the hands is best,

we cannot say. We do know, from study of underwater movies of champion swimmers, that all great swimmers follow the general pattern of those shown in the illustrations on page 5.

STRAIGHT OR BENT ELBOW PULL?

When performing the arm pulls of the various strokes, should the elbows be straight or bent?

When watching the arm action of champion swimmers from out of the water, the arms can be seen to enter the water with the elbows straight and then can be seen to leave the water with the elbows almost straight and in a line almost directly in back of the point at which they entered. One might conclude from this evidence that the swimmer has pulled his arms through the water with a straight elbow and in a straight line directly downward and backward. If a person were to put on a face plate and go underwater to watch the pull of good swimmers, he would find that this is not the case. Instead he would see that they pull in an elliptical or zigzag pattern, as previously described, and *also that they bend their elbows.*

Why is it important that we understand what the swimmers are really doing and the reasons for doing it? Why am I emphasizing the importance of this particular movement or action? Because, if you do not understand why the swimmer should bend his elbow during the pull, you may consciously try to pull with a straight elbow and might recommend the technique to other people.

It can definitely be stated that the swimmer should never, when performing any swimming stroke, pull his arms through the water with a straight arm, that is, with no bend in the elbow. This type of pull is uneconomical. It applies the force in a large semicircular sweeping movement and the resultant reaction is to push the body in the opposite direction and in a circular pattern. Try it and find out for yourself: lie in the water on your back and, using one arm only in a back crawl stroke with the other arm held at the side, pull with a straight arm pull. You will find yourself being pushed around in a circle.

When performing all swimming strokes, the swimmer should begin his arm pull with the elbow straight, or nearly so. As he pulls his arms backward, he should start to bend his elbows. The amount of elbow bend should increase as the pull is made; when the pull is half completed, the elbow bend should reach a maximum flexion of about 90°. During the last half of the pull the elbow bend should decrease until the arm is once again fully (or almost fully) extended. The most descriptive term for the arm pull of all swimming strokes should be "straight-bent-straight" pull.

Figure 1 shows this variation of the elbow bend for the four competitive strokes. This type of pull permits the propulsive force of the arms to be directed backward at a desirable angle and still permits the hands to be pulled in the elliptical pattern described previously.

THE ELBOW-UP POSITION DURING THE PULL

It is important not only that the elbow be bent but also that it be held high during the first part of the pull. In observing underwater movies of poor swimmers and comparing them with movies of such great swimmers as Mark Spitz, Tim Shaw, and others, one very noticeable difference becomes apparent in their arm pulls. The great swimmers carry their elbows high during the first half of the pull (Fig. 2A); the poor crawl swimmers either drop their elbows, as shown in Fig. 2B, or keep their elbows straight as in Fig. 2C.

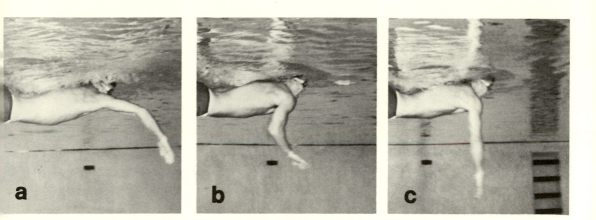

FIG. 2   *Three Types of Elbow Position*
    a. The high elbow
    b. The dropped elbow
    c. The straight elbow

The methods used by poor swimmers result in a wasteful application of force, whereas the high elbow pull permits the swimmers to apply force in the most economical manner. To achieve this high elbow position, you must bend your elbow (described previously) as you rotate your upper arm medially. To understand medial rotation of the upper arms, place your arms directly in front of you at chest height—elbows straight—and with the palms held together. While keeping the thumbs in contact with one another, rotate your arms so the palms face the ground. This medial rotation must occur primarily in the upper arms or the humerus bone as it rotates in the shoulder joint in order to be effective. Do not turn the hands over merely by rotating the lower arms. Try the same action again, but this time, instead of keeping the elbows straight, bend them about 90° as in a praying position (Fig. 3A). Then rotate the arms again in the same manner as

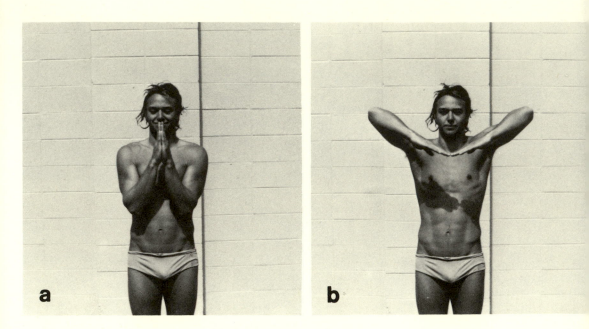

FIG. 3   *Medial Rotation of the Upper Arms*
    a. Place hands in front of the face in praying
position with the elbows at the sides.
    b. Keeping the finger tips together, lift the
elbows up and away from the body.

before, concentrating on lifting the elbows up and away from the body, keeping the wrists straight and permitting only the fingertips to touch, not the palms (Fig. 3B).

This arm action is desirable for all the swimming strokes. Its application in four competitive strokes is shown in Fig. 4.

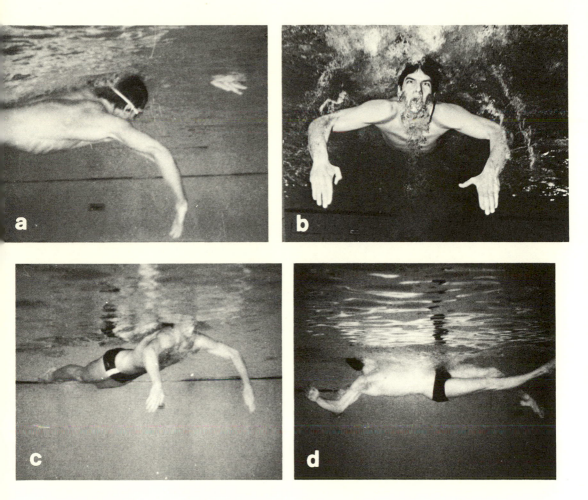

FIG. 4 *Elbow-Up Action during the First Part of the Pull*

   a. Crawl stroke

   b. Butterfly stroke

   c. Breaststroke

   d. Backstroke*

*Because the swimmer's body position is inverted in the backstroke, the elbow action cannot be referred to as "high elbow" even though it is the same as in the other three strokes.

HAND POSITION

Two factors that concern the efficient use of the hands in the water are common to all swimming strokes. These are the angle of entry of the hand into the water, which should be made neatly and without creating too many air bubbles and, second, the way the hand is pulled through the water, that is, whether it is flat or cupped and whether the fingers are held tightly together or spread apart.

ANGLE OF ENTRY

When observing great swimmers in underwater movies, we find that they pull practically no air bubbles after their hands. Beginning and poor swimmers create tremendous swirls of air that follow their hands throughout the pull. This air-water mixture in back of the hands decreases the efficiency of the pull, since it is a less dense medium than water alone. This brief explanation may not satisfy all readers, but to explain more scientifically the reasons that air bubbles decrease the efficiency of the pull would involve the application of some laws of fluid mechanics outside the scope of this book. I hope this brief explanation plus your confidence that I have explored this question thoroughly will be sufficient. Then you can assume that the formation of air bubbles is detrimental. To diminish their number you must place your hands into the water pitched at an angle that is parallel with the line of flight which they were traveling during recovery.

POSITION OF THE HANDS AND FINGERS DURING THE PULL

Should the hand be held flat or cupped with the fingers together or apart? No effort should be made to cup the hand or even to hold the fingers together rigidly. The hand should be held flat so it presents the greatest possible surface area. Cupping the hands was once a recommended method, but, since it decreases the surface area of the hand and therefore decreases pulling efficiency, I don't recommend it.

Should the fingers be held tightly together? When studying underwater movies of great swimmers, we find that during most of the pull their fingers are held together, but that sometimes they do separate slightly, this being particularly true of the thumb. In the case of Mark Spitz, when he swims butterfly or crawl the thumb at times is held at almost a right angle to the rest of the fingers. I do not think there is any difference between the amount of propulsion derived from a hand with the fingers held slightly apart and that derived from a hand with the fingers held closely together. When pulling your hand through the water I think the fingers should not be spread intentionally or held together intentionally. Either action will cause undue tension in the muscles and will inhibit movement of the wrist. If you try to hold your hands in a flat position and keep your fingers close together without overemphasizing that they be forced tightly together, I think you will attain the right hand position. I believe that, as your hands enter the water following the recovery, the fingers should be held together. If they are open, they will pull more air bubbles under the water with them.

DO NOT MAKE SWIMMING MECHANICS TOO COMPLEX

Any person must be able to separate the important aspects from the relatively unimportant. The little things will usually take care of themselves. In swimming, as in other matters, important things should come first. I can give you a good example of a detail man who missed the point by emphasizing irrelevancies and ignoring the relevant. This was a father who was coaching his son to swim the crawl stroke. The boy swam up and down the pool using a dropped elbow—a terrible stroke flaw—yet his father didn't mention it. He kept harping to the boy that he was pulling his hands through the water with the thumbs held out. When I asked the father why he kept at this minor detail, he replied that he was a perfectionist and everything had to be just right. He hoped ultimately to develop the perfect stroke in his boy. In such a plan little details like a closed hand were important. The big problem with perfectionists is that their personality type often includes the inability to discern the important from the unimportant. This is the reason I have mentioned only a few principles in this chapter, but they are the crucial ones in swimming efficiently.

There is another reason. People can think of only a few things at a time when learning a new skill. Crowd their minds with complex instructions and, in the case of swimming, their stroke mechanics will be synthetic and stilted and their learning will be inhibited.

MUCH LEARNING OCCURS NATURALLY

Ask great athletes how they perform their specific sport skill and they will often as not be unable to give you a good description of the mechanics they use. Why is this true? If they were not taught good form and they did not figure it out on the basis of physical laws, why do they perform their movements with such skill?

The answer is fairly simple. They have learned through a trial-and-error process. While this process of learning was going on, they were not always aware of what or how they were learning. If they were throwing a ball, they learned to associate a successful throw with certain sensations in their bodies regarding the position of the hand at the point of release of the ball, the movement of the legs, and so on. If they were swimmers, they learned to associate swimming fast through the water with certain arm positions, the degree of bend in the elbow, and so on. This learning process is primarily neuromuscular in nature and at a subconscious level; it usually proceeds with little direction from the brain in terms of thinking out the movement.

Sometimes, however, you can give the learning process a little help by directing your movements with your thought processes in a very general way—for example, by checking to see if you are bending the elbow as described previously or by concentrating on the medial rotation of the upper arm so the arm will be carried in the high elbow position.

The point I want to make is that you should not direct your movements in a rigid, premeditated manner. Give yourself a general stroke pattern to follow, but permit your natural coordination some freedom to seek out a stroke technique that is best adapted to your strength and body type. Although there is no precise blueprint for stroke mechanics that will fit everyone, certain principles must be observed for a person to be efficient in the water. It is an accepted fact that there are individual anatomical differences that make slight variations in stroke mechanics desirable and sometimes even necessary. For example, a crawl swimmer with poor shoulder flexibility will have to use a wider, more sweeping recovery than will a more flexible swimmer. The fact that there are minor variations in stroke mechanics, however, does not mean that any swimmer can violate mechanical principles and still swim world-class times or even become a good swimmer.

2. Learning to Swim

NOWADAYS, with so many swimming pools and so many people engaging in water sports such as boating, fishing, and water skiing, learning to swim is almost a must. Many people learn in classes, but a survey of the freshman classes at Indiana University showed that many of these people learned to swim, as I did, on their own.

This book can serve as your guide, but, of course, if you get into trouble, it cannot help you as an instructor would. Therefore, you must observe the following safety precautions:

1. Never swim in an unsupervised area. The best place to learn is in shallow water in a swimming pool with a lifeguard on duty.

2. Know your capabilities and your limitations. Don't go into deep water, the surf, a lake, pond, or river until you are certain you can handle the emergencies that may develop.

An aspiring young writer once asked the famous author Ernest Hemingway how he could learn to be a good writer. Hemingway's reply was this: "Write and then write some more." The same advice holds true for learning to swim. To be a good swimmer you must swim and then swim some more. Nearly all physical skills are learned through this trial-and-error process. In this book I hope to guide you through this process in order that you may learn faster and avoid many of the mistakes you would make if you were your own teacher.

ADJUSTMENT TO WATER

At first, you will be a bit afraid of the water. This fear will leave as soon as you can master breath control, can submerge your entire body in the water and keep your eyes open, and can get your feet off the bottom and float.

Don't be too embarrassed, while learning to swim, to take this book along with you as a sort of do-it-yourself guide. You will learn faster if you get in the water often and try the skills many times. You are no different from the thousands of people I have taught to swim. It's really up to you. The magic wand of learning is how many times you get in the water, how hard you work while you are there, and how carefully you follow the instructions.

I have often heard it said and seen it written that it takes a long time to learn to swim. I disagree. In a little over a year after I learned to swim, I earned a high school letter for swimming. You too can learn to swim in a short period of time if you concentrate your efforts, get in the water every day—or at least five times a week—and really work at it.

That doesn't mean that you should rush the learning process. Be patient and keep trying. Progress will usually come at a steady rate with an occasional spurt or plateau. I promise you that not much progress will come with erratic, inconsistent, and halfhearted effort.

One of the feelings you will encounter when you first go into the water is the rush of water into your nose and eyes. You will soon adjust your response to this sensation and your discomfort will disappear. Perhaps a short description here will give you a better idea of what is happening and will speed your adaptation to these two sensations. When you place your head under water, the pressure of the water outside your nose and mouth is greater than the pressure of the air inside. As a result, the water enters the mouth and nose and chokes the beginner. A good way to prevent this experience is to keep your mouth closed when your head is under water and to exhale a small amount of air constantly through your nose. You should be able to feel the bubbles trickle out of your nose. Later on, as you become more accustomed to the water, you will be able to balance the pressure inside your nose and mouth so it is equal to the pressure outside and then no water will enter.

When your head is out of water, inhale through your mouth, but as soon as your head is placed under water, close your mouth and emphasize exhaling through the nostrils.

Remember to keep your eyes open. At first, the rush of water into your eyes will result in blinking, a tendency that we all follow when anything contacts our eyes. You must learn to tolerate this slight discomfort, which seems so irritating at first. In a few exposures to the water and with constant attention to keeping your eyes open, you will soon do so without thinking about it.

The following drills will help you master the adjustment skills. When you have mastered them, you will be ready to learn the flutter kick and, from that point, you will be able to learn the swimming strokes.

Fig. 5   Bobbing under Water

Drill 1. *Bobbing under Water*

Grasp the edge of the pool in water about chest deep. Take a normal breath through your mouth, then bend your knees and drop your entire body, submerging your head. Concentrate on (1) keeping your eyes open (look at your arms and feet), (2) exhaling through your nose (keep a constant stream of air bubbles coming from your nose).

Bring your head back above the surface of the water, but do not remove your hands from the side of the pool—you will be inclined to remove them to wipe the water from your face. Keep your eyes open—you will want to blink them as they are coming out of the water, but you should concentrate on keeping them open.

The first time you try this bobbing action, do it only two or three times, then take a half-minute break and try again, increasing the number of times you bob out of water to three, four, and up until you can bob at least ten times. Then try equalizing the air pressure in the lungs with that of the water by holding your breath while your head is under water. In other words, do not exhale, but hold your breath without letting any air trickle out of your nose. As soon as you have achieved this you will be ready for the second drill.

DRILL 2. *The Prone or Jellyfish Float*

With your lungs inflated, there is a 99 percent chance that you will float at the surface if you keep your head submerged. Not everyone can float on his back with his head out of water, but nearly everyone can stay afloat using the following drill:

A. Stand in water chest deep, lean forward.

FIG. 6   The Prone or Jellyfish Float

B. Submerge your head slowly, pull your feet up from the pool bottom, clasp your knees, keeping your eyes open and holding your breath to a count of 5, 10, or even longer.

C. Regain starting position by extending your knees and lifting your head out of water.

Important. There will be a tendency to lift your feet from the bottom of the pool before submerging your head. This will cause you to sink to the bottom. Instead, observe the following sequence:

1. Take a deep breath, then, while your feet are still in contact with the bottom of the pool, submerge your head completely under water at a slow but steady rate.

2. Now lift your feet off the bottom and pull your knees halfway up to your chest. Repeat this drill until you are thoroughly familiar with it and until you can hold your breath for at least a count of 15.

This is a multipurpose drill: you get your head under water, you practice keeping your eyes open, you learn to inhale, to exhale, and to hold your breath, but, most important, you become aware of the fact that the water will hold you up (buoyancy) and you get accustomed to having your feet off the bottom. This drill also prepares you for the next, which is to learn the prone glide and a method of regaining the vertical or standing position from the swimming or horizontal position.

There are some other drills you can try that have the same purpose as the first two, that is, submersion, keeping the eyes open, breath control, and getting your feet off the bottom.

1. Submerge your head under water, keeping your eyes open, and hold your hand in front of your face under water and count your fingers.

2. Submerge and try to lie on the bottom of the pool.

3. Have a friend stand in the water with his legs spread and see if you can submerge and go between his legs.

4. Throw an object on the bottom of the pool, submerge, and recover the object.

When you can go through these drills easily, you are ready to progress to the next, which is the prone glide.

DRILL 3. *The Prone Glide*

In order to move through the water effectively with any swim-

FIG. 7   The Prone Glide

ming stroke, you must be able to assume and be comfortable in the water in a horizontal position.

Fig. 7A. Standing on one leg in water waist to chest deep, place your arms in front of your face, one hand on top of the other, facing away from the wall. Place one foot against the wall about two and a half feet from the bottom.

Fig. 7B. Submerge your face and arms under water and push hard with the foot you have placed against the wall. If you have pushed hard your body will glide horizontally for ten or fifteen feet. Be sure to keep your body in a straight line by stretching it out from hands to feet.

Fig. 7C. To regain your footing, bring your knees forward and pull your hands downward and back, and go into the jellyfish float position.

Fig. 7D. Then extend your knees and lift your head out of water.

Repeat this drill many times, trying to glide a little further each time. If you are in a narrow pool, you can try to make it all the way across.

If you don't have a pool wall to push against, do the prone glide in the following manner.

DRILL 4. *The Prone Glide (Non-Pool Method)*

A. Stand on one leg with that knee slightly bent and your arms extended forward.

FIG. 8   The Prone Glide (Non-Pool Method)

B. Extend the other leg in back and rock forward, lifting the first leg until both legs are parallel and you are in the glide position.

Before you go to the next step, be certain you do the drills I have discussed. Remember that *repetition* is an important law of learning. I have taught a lot of people to swim and have experimented with different methods a long time before coming up with these progressions as being the best. If you are a quick learner and have little fear of the water, you will do the drills easily and quickly. If it takes you longer to master them, that's all right too. Just don't skip them. The word used for these exercises is *drill;* this term implies that you are going to do them over and over until you have learned them so well that you can do them almost without thinking.

THE FLUTTER KICK

The flutter kick is used with the crawl stroke and with the back crawl stroke. When performing the flutter kick, there are three points to think about:

1. Keep your feet and toes extended. Your toes should be pointed like those of a ballet dancer when she is standing on her toes.

2. Keep your knees straight and kick from your hips. Do not bend your knees. (In reality the knees bend slightly on the down beat when performing the crawl kick and on the up beat when performing the back crawl kick. The beginner, however, should try to keep the knees completely straight. If he tries to bend them even slightly, he will probably bend them too much.)

3. Make the tempo of your kick fast, allowing a separation of about one foot between your feet when they are the furthest apart.

The kick should be first practiced out of water, sitting on the edge of the pool.

FIG. 9   Dry-Land Practice of the Flutter Kick

DRILL 5. *Dry-land Practice of the Flutter Kick*
    A. Point your toes.
    B. Keep your knees straight.
    C. Kick up and down with a fast tempo.
    D. Allow a maximum of twelve inches of spread between your
feet.

DRILL 6. *Stationary Kick on the Wall*
    A. Grasp the top edge of the pool with one hand and, in a line

FIG. 10   Stationary Kick on the Wall

directly underneath it, place the other hand down low on the wall of the pool.

B. Pull with the top hand and push with the bottom hand until your feet are at the surface.

C. Kick with the flutter kick for ten seconds, concentrating on the three points emphasized in Drill 5.

DRILL 7. *Flutter Kick with Glide*

After you have practiced the kick with the two drills above, you are ready to try the flutter kick with the prone glide. This drill will help you evaluate whether you are getting any propulsion out of your kick. If you do not move forward when you are kicking, check to make sure you are doing the kick correctly.

A. Push off the wall of the pool as in Drill 3.

B. When your forward progress from the push-off begins to slow, begin kicking as in Drill 6, remembering to point your toes, keep your knees straight, and kick with a fast tempo and a narrow spread.

FIG. 11   Flutter Kick with Glide

When you have mastered the prone glide and flutter kick, you are ready to progress to the crawl stroke. The crawl stroke arm action and breathing are described in Chapter 3. At this point you are also ready to learn the other swimming strokes. Therefore, I want to suggest a way of devising your lesson plans in the best way to learn and perfect the various strokes.

To my way of thinking it is better to give you guidelines rather than rigid plans that do not take into consideration the differences among individuals. Some of you may be more advanced in skill to begin with and the rate of progress may vary widely.

Here are some suggestions concerning the planning of a practice session.

SUGGESTIONS FOR PLANNING A PRACTICE SESSION

Plan each session just as a champion would plan his workouts. Outline each segment of the session in a manner similar to the one below:

1. (Two to five minutes.) Get into the water and move around until you get accustomed to the water temperature. If you are a beginner and haven't learned any skills, just wade around in the shallow end of the pool, splash the water with your hands, get your hair and face wet. If you have been in the water a number of times before and have been following the instructions in this book, practice the skills you have learned in previous sessions, such as bobbing, the jellyfish float, the prone glide with the flutter kick, and so on.

2. (Five to ten minutes.) Review the previous drills and repeat the skills you have started to learn. If you are a goal-oriented and well-organized person, you will want to review them in the order in which they were learned.

3. (Ten to twenty minutes.) Spend this time in learning the new skills to which you are about to be introduced. Follow the book carefully.

4. If you have time left over, spend it practicing and improving skills already learned. Try kicking or swimming a little further than you have gone before. Develop a feel for all your skills. If you do them often, their performance will become automatic.

All the time you are practicing, you will also be improving your physical conditioning. You will be developing strength and endurance and learning muscular coordination and relaxation. You will be developing confidence and losing any fear of the water you may have felt.

SAMPLE PRACTICE SESSION

Assuming it took three practice sessions to master the skills discussed earlier in this chapter, you are now ready to follow the next two. They are designed to help you work into the practice of making up your own session plans. You are the best judge of the state of your progress and, since this method of learning is based on learning by doing, it is unnecessary to make rigid plans which are based on drills.

Session 4. The Crawl Stroke

A. Try the crawl stroke as described in Chapter 3.

B. Practice some bobbing drills, concentrating on keeping your eyes open, exhaling through your nose, and inhaling through your mouth.

C. Practice the flutter kick and prone glide, then go back to trying the whole stroke. This time, try to work in a breathing pattern.

Session 5. Review

Review all the skills you have learned and continue to work on the crawl stroke. Your emphasis should be to improve your breathing pattern.

After Session 5 continue to outline and plan your practice sessions, referring to other chapters which deal with the other strokes—the butterfly, back crawl, and breaststroke. Try to master as many skills as you can, taking up one skill or stroke at a time and working it into the session plan. If you feel you have not sufficiently mastered the skill of the previous session, repeat it, but do not try to perfect it. Perfection will come only gradually. Do not repeat a whole lesson completely more than once or you will lose the challenge. If you get hung up on a particular skill, go on to other skills and come back to the bothersome part later.

One of the most common errors people make in learning to swim is to stay with the particular stroke that has been the easiest to acquire. They limit their ultimate swimming skill by putting a ceiling on their potential. To fully enjoy swimming, to exercise more muscles, and to achieve more variety and challenge, you should learn and try to master at least three swimming strokes.

A good friend of mine followed the general outline I have presented here and learned to swim at the age of thirty-five. At age thirty-six she entered a Masters swimming meet and swam the 1500-meter swim in about 30 minutes. I mention this to show you what can be done with practice and determination. You can do the same or even better, but you must accept the challenge and practice regularly, always following instructions carefully.

Another suggestion to consider: two, three, or more people learning together can easily follow this book, teaching, evaluating, and encouraging one another.

THE USE OF ARTIFICIAL FLOATS

There are many different kinds of artificial floats on the market today
that are used to support the swimmer and prevent him going under
water. They provide the swimmer with confidence to try the different
strokes without fear.

Some of them are helpful, but some are dangerous and some
impede or even prevent correct learning. I will not try to discuss
individual devices, since they are so many and varied, but I can tell
you what to look for and what to avoid if you want to purchase one of
them.

Certain swimming aids, such as the inner-tube type, prevent the
swimmer from learning to swim with his head submerged. Such learning devices as tubes and other extremely large flotation aids that
prevent a person from getting his head under water when he is wearing
them cause the person to float in a very high position and should be
avoided. Secondly, all aids are hazardous to the extent that they provide false security. The wearer may move into deep water and slip out
of the support or it may become deflated due to a leaky valve or a hole
being torn in it.

Here are a few things to look for when buying a swimming aid:

1. The aid should fasten securely around the swimmer with a
fastener that cannot easily become loose or disengaged.

2. The aid should be non-inflatable so that air leaks are not a
possibility.

3. The aid should not prevent the swimmer from submerging his
head or from assuming a horizontal position in the water.

It may be useful to note here that these factors should also be considered when buying a safety aid for a non-swimming child. The parent of a non-swimming child is rightly worried about the child being around the water. He will often purchase an inflatable, inner-tube type of support that will keep the child's head high out of the water. Now he feels less anxious and with his mind relieved takes his attention from the child. Two things are wrong with this reasoning: the vulnerability of such a device to air leakage and the false sense of confidence it gives both the child and the parent. The parent would be well advised to observe the standards given above when he purchases a safety device for a non-swimming child.

3. The Crawl Stroke

THE CRAWL STROKE is the fastest and most efficient of the competitive swimming strokes. In freestyle races a swimmer may swim any style he wishes; in nearly every case the crawl is the stroke that is chosen. Whether a swimmer is swimming an all-out sprint for maximum speed or swimming a great distance such as the English Channel, the crawl is the stroke that gets him there the fastest.

The world record for men for 100 meters in each of the four competitive strokes is shown below to give you an idea of the comparative speeds for these strokes:

Event	Time	Swimmer	Country
Freestyle	49.44 secs.	Jonty Skinner	South Africa
Butterfly	54.27 secs.	Mark Spitz	U.S.A.
Backstroke	55.49 secs.	John Naber	U.S.A.
Breaststroke	63.11 secs.	John Hencken	U.S.A.

You cannot consider yourself an accomplished swimmer until you have mastered the crawl stroke. Before I learned to swim I used to picture myself swimming a powerful crawl stroke just like Johnny Weissmuller did in his popular Tarzan movies. When I finally did learn to swim the crawl stroke efficiently and was swimming it in high school meets, the feeling I got was just as I had imagined it would be. Even today, as a coach, I swim about two miles a day, most of it crawl stroke. I still get that enjoyable feeling of rhythm and power as I go through the water. Some people get this same thrill when they ski, ice-skate, play tennis, or participate in some other sports activity. Many people get this feeling when they swim. This book should help you acquire enough skill to enjoy swimming as much as I do. Let's work together to achieve that goal.

You may someday stand on the victor's stand at the Olympic Games, but even if you never compete in a swimming race, you will get the great feeling of unity with the water and you will swim for pleasure and health for the rest of your life. A good friend of mine is eighty-five years old and she swims several hundred yards a day, six days a week, most of it in crawl stroke.

In Chapters 1 and 2 the crawl stroke was mentioned briefly. While I didn't go into great detail, I did suggest certain drills that will help you prepare for the crawl stroke. My plan now is to go into greater detail in describing the various movements of the crawl. Even if you are a successful competitive swimmer, you should take a look at this chapter as a guide to improve your stroke.

BODY POSITION

The body should be in a flat or streamlined position.

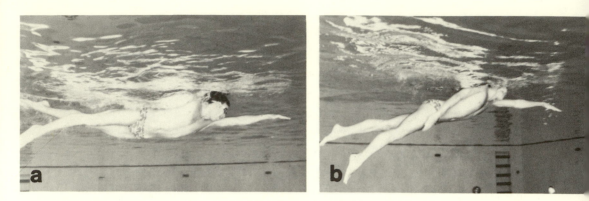

FIG. 12   *Body Position*
 a. *Good body position.* The body is flat or streamlined. The breath is taken by turning the head to the side. The kick is efficient, keeping the hips up.
 b. *Poor body position.* The body is not flat, but is carried at an angle. The breath is taken in front by lifting the head, thus causing the hips to drop. The kick is poor and fails to support the hips.

If you swim with your head held too high or if your kick is not efficient, you will not be able to swim in a streamlined or flat body position.

Your hips should be high enough in the water so they are just below the surface. Have someone watch you as you swim and ask him to notice how much under the water level your hips are. If they are more than a few inches beneath the surface, you must improve your kick or correct your head position.

THE FLUTTER KICK

The most efficient kick is the flutter kick, which consists of kicking the

legs up and down with the knees almost straight and the toes pointed or
extended. The width of the kick—separation of the feet—should be
about twelve inches at the widest point. The main job of the kick is to
hold your body in a streamlined position, and the best way to practice
the kick is with the use of a *kickboard*. Kickboards are usually made
from foam plastic and are available at many sporting-goods stores.
They are an important piece of equipment for the beginning, advanced,
or competitive swimmer. At Indiana University our swimming team
practices kicking at least twenty minutes a day. This means that each
swimmer kicks about a half mile or more a day. This type of drill is
important in developing good conditioning for the leg muscles as well
as in developing the proper form.

When holding the board in front of you, grasp it on the side and
do not press it downward, but stretch it out in front of you, keeping
your shoulders low in the water and the body horizontal. Don't kick
your feet out of the water, but let the heels and soles come just to the

FIG. 13 *Using the Kickboard.* Stretching the board in front of him, the swimmer does
not press downward. He keeps his shoulders low in the water and his hips close to the surface.

surface and churn the water. Not only beginners but even some advanced swimmers let the whole foot break the surface of the water, thus decreasing the effectiveness of their kick.

FOOT POSITION

When doing the flutter kick, your toes should be pointed or extended, as if you were a ballet dancer and were dancing on your toes.

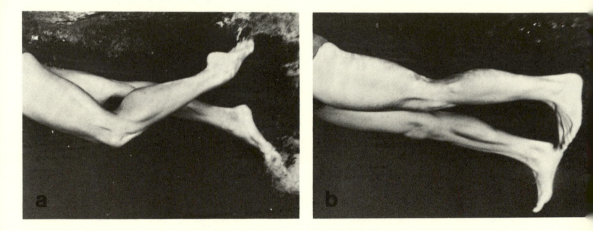

FIG. 14   *Good and Poor Foot Position during the Flutter Kick*
   a. Good foot position, with the toes pointed.
   b. Poor foot position, with the foot hooked.

If you are not making enough forward progress when you kick on the board, it is likely due to one of two things: either your feet are not pointed or extended enough or you are bending your knees too much. I have seen swimmers who actually remain stationary when they kick on a board. If this happens to you, check to see that you are not using a hooked foot as shown in Fig. 14B. Try stretching your ankles with the exercise shown in Fig. 15, as many competitive swimmers do who want to improve their ankle flexibility.

KNEE BEND

The second mistake you may make when doing the flutter kick is to bend your knees too much.

The knees should be bent only slightly and then only on the down beat. *Since most people tend to bend the knees too much when practicing the kick, you will probably do so too. You should make a great effort to keep your knees almost completely straight and to kick from the hips.*

FIG. 15 *Exercise to Improve Ankle Flexibility*. Sit on your heels with the top of your foot placed on the floor. Lift your knees and rock backward.

a

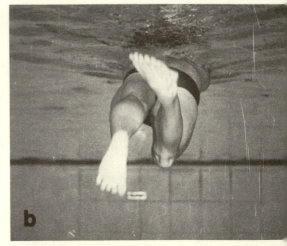

b

c

d

e

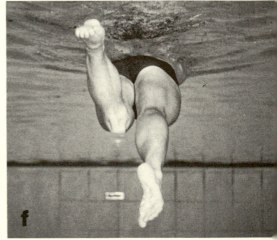

f

FIG. 16 (OPPOSITE)   *A Flutter Kick Sequence As Seen from Directly in Back*
a. The left leg has just finished its down beat and the right foot is at the top of its movement.
b. The left leg starts upward with the knee straight. The right leg starts downward with the knee bent.
c & d. The left leg continues upward with the knee straight, while the right leg continues downward with the knee bent.
e. The left foot continues upward as the right knee starts down. This action is accomplished by bending the knee. The final downward thrust of the right foot is accomplished by extension of the knee.
f. The left leg has completed its upward movement and the knee is bent. The right leg is at the bottom of its movement and the knee is straight. The next kick is ready to begin.

POINTS TO REMEMBER WHEN PRACTICING THE FLUTTER KICK
1. Point or extend your feet.
2. Keep your knees almost completely straight.
3. Kick from the hips.
4. Let the heels of your feet just break the surface.
5. Keep your body flat and close to the surface.

You can best improve your kick by doing kicking drills on the kickboard. Kick several lengths of the pool today, do more tomorrow and even more the next day. If you can't go very far at one time before you tire and stop moving forward, rest a half minute or so and start again. Remember that you learn by doing, so keep trying to go a little further and a little faster each day, even if you have to stop occasionally to let your legs rest.

THE ARM STROKE

A way to describe the crawl arm stroke might be to say that it looks like the pedals of a bicycle in action—one arm (or pedal) is pulling under the body and through the water, while the other is recovering over the water and getting ready for the next stroke.

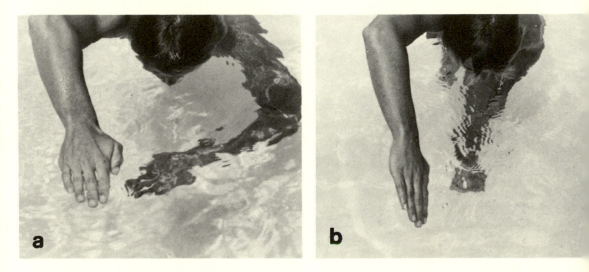

FIG. 17   *Pitch of the Hands*
   a. *Incorrect placement of the hand as it enters the water.* The hands should not enter the water with the palms flat. This will cause air bubbles to be captured and pulled along with the hand and will make the arm pull less efficient.
   b. *Correct placement of the hand as it enters the water.* The hands should enter the water with the thumb first and the hand pitched at 45° from the horizontal. The pitched entry will prevent air bubbles from following the hand entry.

You can't really compare the action of the pedal and the arm because the pedal is rigid and has a fixed path, while your arm makes its own path. The pedal always does the right thing, while your arm can make mistakes. It's up to you to choose the correct path for your arm, and the rest of this chapter is planned to help you do so, not only with the arm pull, but with the rest of your stroke.

PITCH OF THE HANDS

If the hand is placed into the water in a flat position, as in Fig. 17A, it will pull air bubbles after it, which will decrease the efficiency of the arm pull. The hand should be placed in the water so the thumb enters the water first and the hand is pitched at a 45° angle, as in Fig. 17B. In this manner the hand enters the water without pulling air bubbles with it.

After the hand has entered the water, the palm should be turned down to face the bottom of the pool. This action is accompanied by rotation of the forearm.

THE ARM PULL

The arm pull of all good swimmers follows a zigzag pattern under their bodies and your arm pull should do so as well. As your hand goes into the water your arm should be almost straight and directly above your shoulder. As you pull your arm under your body, you should bend your elbow more and more until it forms a 90° angle when the arm is halfway through the pull.

If you were lying on the bottom of the pool and watching yourself swim over you and, if you were pulling correctly, you would see the following:

1. Each hand would be making an upside-down question mark pattern as it pulled down and back under the body.

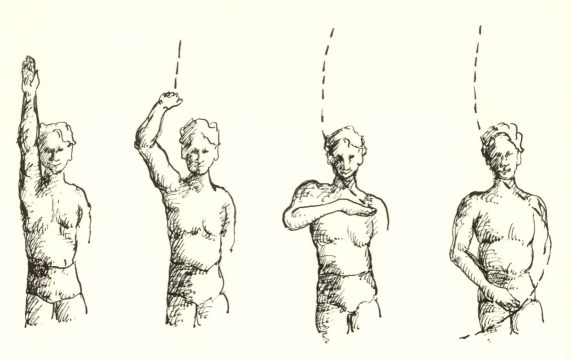

FIG. 18   *Pull Pattern and Elbow Action*
    a. The arm pull begins with the elbow straight or almost straight. As soon as the swimmer begins to pull he starts to bend the elbow.
    b. As the first half of the pull is made the elbow continues to bend until the pull is half completed.
    c. At this point the elbow is bent approximately 90°.
    d. During the last half of the pull the elbow extends as the hand pushes backward to a point below the hips.

      2. The greatest amount of elbow bend would come when your hand was under your shoulder and when your arm pull was half completed.

      3. You would be finishing your pull with your elbow almost straight and your hand below your hips or at the bottom of your swimsuit.

      As you pull your arms through the water, try to feel constant

FIG. 19 *Elbow-Up Pull.* The high elbow action of four Olympians is shown from slightly different angles.

    a. Jenny Turrall, world record holder in the 1500-meter freestyle, as seen from the side.

    b. Jennifer Hooker as seen from a diagonal angle. Notice the entry of the other hand with the palm facing diagonally sidewards.

    c. Jim Montgomery, 100-meter Olympic champion and former world record holder is shown from head on.

    d. Olympic champion and world record holder Kornelia Ender is shown carrying her elbow very high during the first part of the crawl arm pull. Her arm pull pattern is slightly wider than that of most swimmers.

pressure on the palms of your hands. This constant pressure gives you the sense of power and rhythm I mentioned before. The force created by the pressure of your hands pushing against the water is what propels you through the water. If you don't feel this pressure, you should pull harder and check to see that your arms are pulling in the manner described above.

The elbow-up pull. When I look at underwater movies of such great swimmers as Jim Montgomery, Brian Goodell, and Mark Spitz, I find they have one thing in common: when they swim the crawl stroke, they swim with their elbows held in a high position during the first half of the pull. This permits the hands to push the water more directly backward and is, therefore, more efficient in pulling the body forward.

This high elbow position is accomplished by bending the elbows and pressing the hand downward as the elbow remains almost stationary. This action is accomplished by the medial rotation of the upper arm and by bending the elbow as shown in Figs. 2 and 3. You can do this on dry land and watch this action, which is as though reaching over a barrel. The importance of the high elbow position cannot be overstressed.

The most common mistake that swimmers make is to swim with a dropped elbow. This defect is a sure way of wasting your energy in going nowhere.

FIG. 20   *Dropped Elbow Pull*—a serious stroke defect

Your arm pull should be long, that is, long enough to keep you pushing until your hand is below the bottom of your swimsuit. This will make the arm recovery (the top part of the pedal action) much easier.

Strengthening the pulling muscles. The muscles used to maintain the correct stroke technique—that is, with the high, bent elbow and the long, forceful pulling action—are not strengthened enough by everyday activity. The serious swimmer must use supplementary exercise to strengthen them. Many competitive swimmers use a form of strengthening exercise that simulates the correct arm action of the strokes they swim. Most of the 1976 United States Olympic swimmers use isokinetic exercise. In Fig. 21 Jim Montgomery is doing the crawl stroke arm action drill on the Mini-Gym isokinetic swim bench.

FIG. 21   *Jim Montgomery on the Isokinetic Swim Bench*

FIG. 22 (OPPOSITE) *Crawl Stroke Arm Recovery.* The arm recovery is made after the pull is completed.

    a. As the arm lifts out of the water the elbow is bent slightly.

    b. As the arm swings forward the bend in the elbow increases.

    c. The elbow is carried high and the hand clears, but stays near, the surface of the water.

    d. As the arm reaches forward the elbow begins to extend.

    e. The arm enters the water with the elbow almost fully extended.

FIG. 23 *Correct and Incorrect Arm Recovery Action*

    a. Correct elbow action, in which the elbow is bent and carried high during the arm recovery.

    b. Poor elbow action, in which the elbow is almost straight and the arm swings too wide. This action causes the hips to wiggle.

    c. Poor hand position, in which the hand is carried higher than the elbow.

THE RECOVERY

As your arm pull ends and the recovery begins, your elbow should be almost straight, as you can see in Fig. 22A.

The recovery ends when you place your hand in the water directly in front of your shoulder. As your hand enters the water, your elbow should be only slightly bent. If you swing your arm wide on the recovery phase, as shown in Figs. 23B and 23C, it will cause your hips and legs to wiggle sideways, which will disturb the streamlining of your body.

It is also important that the hand be carried close to the body as it is swung forward in the recovery. The hand should never be lifted much higher than two to three inches above the water (Fig. 22C). I often see swimmers who lift their hand higher than their elbow and I want to tell them they are being inefficient because they are throwing their hips out of line and disturbing their streamlined body position. Always keep in mind that any action that disturbs your streamlining is probably bad.

After reading the brief description of the arm recovery above, look at the illustrations carefully and then try to imitate them in the water. Have someone watch you swim, then have him look at the illustrations to be certain that you are not using a wide arm recovery.

Ask your observer to see if you are recovering your arms in the following manner:

1. With a bent elbow which is carried high.

2. With your hand entering the water directly in front of your shoulder and with the elbow almost straight at this point.

It is impossible to see yourself and you often don't know exactly what you are doing. If you don't have an instructor or coach around, ask a friend or a parent to observe you.

HEAD POSITION

Your head should be held so it is half submerged, the waterline at its middle. You should be looking forward and diagonally down at about a 45° angle. Don't carry your head so high that your eyebrows are out of the water; also avoid carrying your head so low that it is completely submerged except when you are breathing.

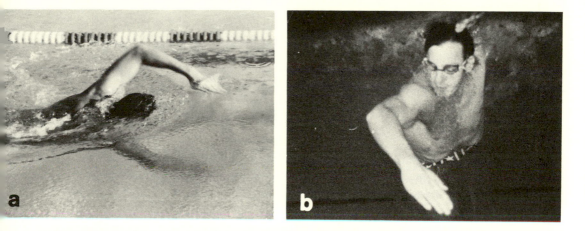

FIG. 24   *Head Position of Olympic Champion Jim Montgomery*
   a. As seen from a side view, out of the water.
   b. As seen from a head-on underwater angle. Notice the waterline in relation to his head.

BREATHING

It is a common misunderstanding to believe that you should breathe on the right side if you are right-handed and on the left side if you are left-handed. Try both sides and breathe on the side that feels the most comfortable.

Take your breath by turning your head to the side through rotation of your neck. The air should be inhaled through your mouth when your hand on your breathing side is at the end of its pull. A very common mistake is one that is termed "late breathing," in which the swimmer takes his breath during the recovery of the arm on the breathing side. You can avoid "late breathing" by starting to turn the head to the side immediately after the arm pull on the breathing side is begun. That is, if you breathe on the right side, you must start to turn your head to the side immediately after your right arm begins to pull down and backward. This will place your head in position to breathe as the right hand finishes its pull. This timing plus the correct placement of the head will enable you to breathe at the bottom of the bow wave, as shown in Fig. 25. As the body moves forward a bow wave is formed in front of the head with a trough or cavity just in back of it. If the swimmer places his head in the correct position, he can breathe at the bottom of this trough.

Blow the air out through both the mouth and the nose in a steady rhythm when your mouth is under water, but take in your breath only through your mouth.

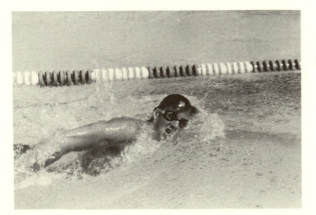

FIG. 25   *Correct Breathing Technique* (Jim Montgomery)

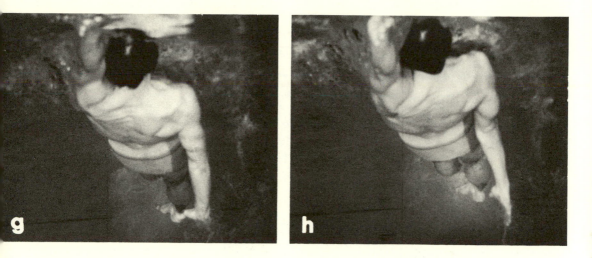

FIG. 42 *Underwater Analysis of Olympian Mike Stamm's Back Crawl.* This sequence of photographs of one complete arm pull shows many of the desirable features discussed in this chapter and should be examined carefully for the following items.

1. *Head position.* The head is held in a position that submerges most of it with only the face being out of the water.
2. *Body roll.* The body rolls approximately 45° to each side. The maximum roll is achieved when the pulling arm has completed half of its pull (e).
3. *Arm action*
   a. The right arm enters the water almost directly overhead as the left arm is being lifted upward. There is no bend in the elbow of either arm.
   b. The right arm sinks about one foot below the surface with no apparent bend in the elbow.
   c. The elbow begins to bend as the arm is pulled down and back.
   d. The elbow bend increases as the arm continues backward.
   e. The elbow reaches maximum bend of 90° as the pull is half completed. The hand is now about one foot below the surface of the water.
   f. The final back and downward push of the hand begins as the elbow begins to extend.
   g. The final push of the hand is made downward as the elbow reaches full extension. The purpose of this downward push is to cause the right shoulder to lift upward.
   h. The right arm begins its recovery upward with the elbow fully extended, the palm facing inward, and the thumb up. The left hand enters the water directly over the shoulder with the little finger entering the water first and the palm facing outward.

FIG. 43 *The "Inverted Elbow-Up" Arm Position of Olympic Champion Ulrike Richter*. This desirable arm position is obtained by bending the elbow and rotating the upper arm medially.

FIG. 44 *Pitch of the Hands in the Back Crawl*. In (a) the hand is entering the water, little finger first and palm facing outward. In (b) the hand is leaving the water, thumb first and the palm facing toward the body. The pitch of the hand at other points in the stroke may be observed in FIG. 42.

pulling much air after them. It also permits them to sink deeper into the water than if they were put in the water flat. There is a tendency for the average swimmer to let his hands enter the water with the palm facing upward. This error should be corrected immediately if you find you are doing it. Have someone watch you for this stroke flaw, since it is almost impossible to see it yourself. During the pull your palm should stay in straight alignment with the forearm, so your wrist should not flex or your forearm rotate.

THE ARM RECOVERY

As each arm recovers it should be brought out of the water with the elbow fully extended and the palm facing inward. Each arm should remain fully extended with no bend in the elbow throughout the entire arm recovery. During its recovery the arm must be rotated laterally in order that the little finger may enter first with the palm facing outward. The recovery of each arm should be made in a straight line in the vertical plane. Deviation sideward from this plane will result in a sideward displacement of the hips and legs and will increase the resistance or drag that the swimmer creates. Figure 45 illustrates the correct arm recovery for the back crawl.

HEAD POSITION AND BREATHING

The head position in the back crawl should be in almost straight alignment with your body, as though you were lying in bed on your back and had no pillow under your head (Fig. 46). If you are very buoyant or have an exceptionally good kick, your head should be tilted forward slightly, as though you were lying in bed and had a small pillow under your head.

FIG. 45   *Back Crawl Arm Recovery.* The out-of-the-water arm action of Olympic champion and world record holder John Naber. The arm is recovered in a vertical plane with no bend in the elbow.

FIG. 46   *Head Position of Olympian John Murphy in the Back Crawl Stroke*

Breathing seems to present no real problem in the back crawl, since you can breathe whenever you desire. One word of advice: do not breathe too often or too shallowly. A good policy is to inhale on the recovery of one arm and exhale on the recovery of the other. In this way you will assure yourself of not panting or taking short, shallow breaths.

TIMING OF THE ARMS AND LEGS

The timing of the legs and arms is such that the swimmer uses six kick beats per complete arm cycle (one pull of each arm). This timing occurs at such a fast rate that you cannot really think of it. Fortunately, you do not have to think about it, since, if you try to swim the stroke as it should be swum, the kick and the arm stroke will find the right coordination without conscious control from you. For this reason it is pointless for me to complicate your learning process by delving into the details of the timing of the pull and kick.

BODY ROLL

Although, when we study movies of champion back crawlers, we find that they roll 90° on the longitudinal axis (45° to each side), you should not try to roll intentionally. You should also not try to inhibit your roll to swim in a flat position with neither shoulder dipping to either side. The amount of body roll shown in Fig. 42 is desirable and is the result of correct arm and leg action, not any conscious effort on the part of the swimmer. The downward push of the hands at the end of the arm pull is one of the main forces that causes body roll and is, therefore, desirable.

FIG. 47 *The Back Crawl Racing Start*

a. At the command ''Swimmers, tak[e] your marks,'' the swimmer pulls him[-] self to the starting block.

b & c. At the sound of the gun the swimmer pushes himself backward a[nd] upward, throwing his arms forward i[n] wide sweeping motion.

d. Immediately before entering the water his body reaches extension wit[h] arms extended overhead.

THE BACK CRAWL RACING START

For a number of years I have been trying to get the competitive swimming rules committees of the various governing bodies to permit the back crawlers to start from a racing dive off the starting blocks, rather than from in the water and with the use of backstroke hand grips as is presently done. Unfortunately, I have been unsuccessful so far. The hand grip is part of the starting block and is so located that the swimmer may grasp it and raise himself partly out of the water so as to overcome some of the resistance of the water. In international and AAU competition the backstroker must keep his feet completely under water and his body at least partially submerged. In high school and college swimming he is permitted to lift as much of his body out of the water as he desires, so long as part of his feet remain under water. There seems to be no advantage to lifting the body completely out of the water and this kind of start is used by very few good swimmers. Figure 47 depicts the back crawl start.

THE BACK CRAWL TURN

If you are racing and concerned with speed, you want to use the back crawl flip or somersault turn. The rules governing the backstroke turn state that you must stay on your back until you touch the end of the pool with one of your hands. You may then turn off your back, but you must once again be on your back before your push-off is completed. Figure 48 illustrates and describes this turn.

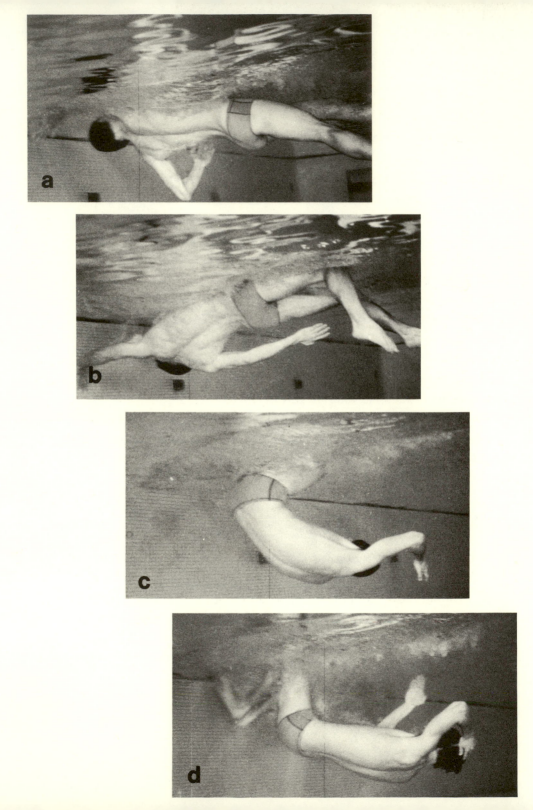

FIG. 48 *The Back Crawl Flip Turn*

a. The swimmer reaches for the wall with his right hand, while the left hand continues its pull.

b. As the swimmer touches the wall he bends his elbow slightly. He throws his knees out of the water and positions his left hand with the palm ready to pull upward toward his head.

c. The legs are thrown over the surface of the water and the left hand continues to pull toward the head. This arm action helps turn the body around.

d. The left hand ends its pulling action with an action in which the swimmer appears to be patting his head. The feet submerge. During the entire turn the swimmer is never off his back.

e. The arms are extended overhead as the feet are planted against the wall about a foot and a half below the surface of the water. The swimmer is now in position to push-off.

f. The swimmer pushes off and holds the glide position momentarily until he slows to swimming speed, when he will begin stroking.

6. The Breaststroke

ALTHOUGH THE BREASTSTROKE is one of the competitive strokes, it is also a good utility stroke that you can use for long, slow, easy distance swimming. It is also a good stroke for use in lifesaving technique. It is the slowest of the four competitive strokes, being over 13 seconds slower for 100 meters than the crawl stroke. The world record for the 100-meter crawl for men is :49.44, while that of the 100-meter breast is :63.11. In the women's 100-meter breaststroke the record is 1:10.87, while the world record for the crawl is :55.65.

The technique as advocated in this chapter and used by good competitive swimmers is essentially the same for recreational and leisure swimmers. If you are just learning to swim the breaststroke or if you are a competitive swimmer who wants to improve technique, you should try to perform the stroke in the manner described in this chapter.

COMPETITIVE RULES GOVERNING THE BREASTSTROKE

The present competitive rules governing the breaststroke events state that the body must be kept perfectly on the breast and the shoulders must be held in the horizontal plane. Both hands must be pushed forward together under water and pulled backward simultaneously and symmetrically. The feet must be pulled up simultaneously and symmetrically with the knees open. During the backward thrust of the legs, the feet must sweep outward and then together. Up-and-down movements of the legs in the vertical plane are prohibited. This eliminates the use of the fishtail kick, as well as the flutter kick or scissors kick. The breaststroke kick—sometimes called the frog kick—is the only one that can conform to these rules.

When touching at the turn or on finishing a race, the touch must be made with both hands at the same time and at the same level. There is a variation to this rule in the high school and college rules that will be discussed later in this chapter.

The swimmer must swim with part of his head out of water at all times except after the start and each turn, when he is permitted one underwater arm pull and kick.

BODY POSITION

This stroke is the one in which the greatest number of swimmers violate the principle of good streamlining by not swimming in a flat

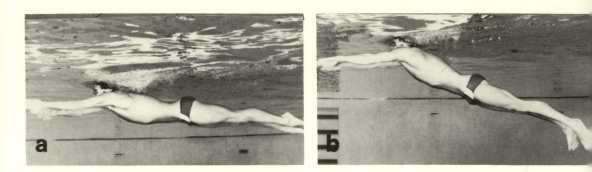

FIG. 49 *Streamlining in the Breaststroke*
a. Good body position
b. Poor body position

position. Figure 49B shows the swimmer moving through the water at a poor angle and creating excessive drag. The poor body position in this case is due to the swimmer carrying his head too high in the water when he is not breathing. In Figure 49A his hips and legs are higher and his body is in a more streamlined position.

Other factors, such as arching the back, improper timing of the breathing, and excessively high lift of the head and shoulders out of the water also result in destroying the desirable planing or streamlining of the body.

THE BREASTSTROKE KICK

The breaststroke kick has undergone some changes in the past twenty years. The wide, wedge kick that was advocated for so long has been replaced by the narrower, whip-action kick for beginners up through competitive swimmers. The terms "wide" and "narrow" are relative and mean nothing unless compared with something else or with a measurement. When using the wide, wedge kick, the feet were separated by at least thirty-six inches and sometimes as much as forty-two inches was recommended. Underwater movies of today's champion swimmers show as little spread as eighteen inches between the feet, although the average spread would be closer to twenty-four inches. Figure 50 illustrates and describes the correct form of the breaststroke kick.

The breaststroke kick should be practiced with kickboard drills for the purposes of improving mechanics, evaluating the effectiveness of your kick, and conditioning your legs. You should stretch the kickboard in front of you and make a strong effort to keep your shoulders low in the water. You should hold the kickboard in the manner shown in Fig. 13.

Be careful to see that your heels do not break the surface of the water as they are brought forward. If they do, you should concentrate on bringing the knees more up and under the hips. This will usually get your heels down under the surface where they belong.

ANKLE FLEXIBILITY

When swimming the three other competitive strokes, it is desirable to have good extention (plantar flexion) of the ankles. That is, you should be able to point your feet and toes the way a ballet dancer does when she makes a toe stand. When swimming breaststroke, however, you need just the opposite kind of flexibility—dorsiflexion.

To learn if you have average, better, or below-average dorsiflexion you can try the following simple test. Stand erect and barefooted with your feet together, the toes and heels of each foot touching one

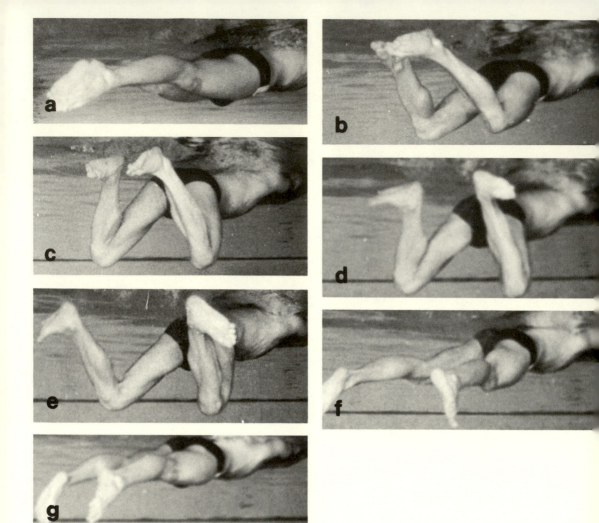

FIG. 50 *The Breaststroke Kick*

    a. The kick begins with the legs and feet fully extended and the hips and legs close to the surfac of the water.

    b. The heels are brought up toward the buttocks by flexion of the hips and legs close to the surface of the water.

    b. The heels are brought up toward the buttocks by flexion of the hips and knees.

    c. As the legs are drawn up, the feet stay close together, but the knees spread.

    d. The ankles flex so the broad surface of the soles of the feet is in good position to thrust the water backward.

    e. A powerful backward thrust of the legs is made as the feet perform a semicircular, sweeping action.

    f. As the legs are squeezed together, the knees continue to extend.

    g. The knees become fully extended immediately before the feet come together. The feet come together as they are shown in (a). They will hold this position momentarily for a short glide.

another and your hands grasped behind your neck. Now execute a full tuck position as in Fig. 51 and let your buttocks drop as close to your heels as you can without permitting your heels to leave the floor. If you have normal flexibility, you will be able to drop all the way to the floor without raising your heels. If you do not and you try to go all the way down, you will either fall backward or your heels will rise. This indicates you need to improve the flexibility of your ankles.

FIG. 51   *Measuring Ankle Flexibility*

Many people have short calf muscles and tight Achilles tendons, which prevent them from having good ankle flexibility and a good breaststroke kick. If you want to improve your flexibility, the exercises shown in Figs. 52 and 53 will help.

THE BREASTSTROKE ARM PULL

The mechanics of the breaststroke arm pull were described briefly in

Chapter 1. If you have not read that presentation or have forgotten some of the material, it would be a good idea to read it again.

The arm pull is made with the hands pressing outward, backward, and downward and, finally, after the maximum width of the pull is achieved (about thirty to forty inches), the hands are brought back toward the center line of the body. Figure 54 shows the pull pattern of

FIG. 52 *Ankle Stretcher*. Lean forward against the wall so your body is at a 45° angle. Push against the wall with your hands and let all of the pressure of your body be placed on the back foot so the heel is forced toward the ground. This action will stretch out your calf (gastrocnemius) muscle. Now, reverse and try it with the other leg. Do this exercise for a few minutes each day, especially before practice or a meet.

FIG. 53 *Ankle Stretcher Exercise on an Inclined Plane*. Grasp the hand grip. Keep the knees bent slightly and pull yourself forward in a gentle rocking motion, placing a stretch on the calf muscle and Achilles tendon. Do this exercise once or twice a day for five minutes at a time. The angle of incline should be about 35° to 45°, depending on the swimmer's ankle flexibility.

a champion breaststroker, as taken from movies from directly below the swimmer.

THE HIGH ELBOW POSITION

When swimming the breaststroke it is important that you maintain the high elbow position during the arm pull, just as was recommended

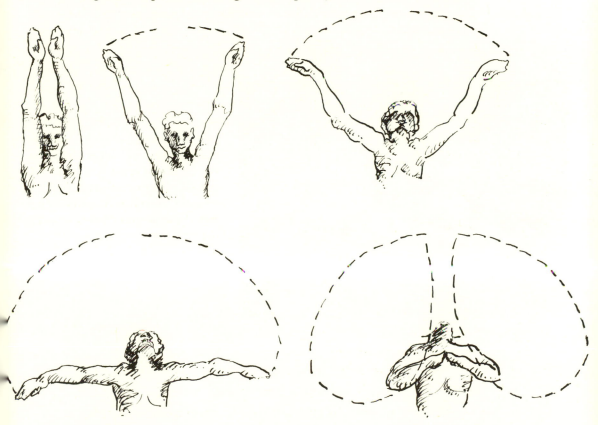

FIG. 54 *The Breaststroke Arm Pull*
    a. The arms are extended forward in the glide position.
    b. The press of the hands starts outward and downward and the elbows begin to bend slightly.
    c. The arms continue to press outward as the elbows increase their bend.
    d. The hands press back as far as the shoulders. The bend of the elbows increases, but the elbows are not pulled into the ribs. The head has lifted for the inhalation.
    e. The pull ends as the hands start forward into the fully extended glide position.

for the butterfly and crawl strokes. This high elbow position permits the best application of force because it enables you to push the water backward in a sculling motion at a desirable angle as you pull.

This action is accomplished by bending your elbows and medially rotating your upper arms as your arms pull backward. Medial rotation of the upper arms is also required to perform the correct mechanics of the other three competitive strokes and has been discussed in earlier chapters. By this time you are probably getting the idea that I think it is important. Figure 55 shows this high elbow position.

FIG. 55 *Elbow-Up Pull*. The pull is pictured as the hands are pressed outward and backward. The high elbow is maintained by bending the elbow and medially rotating the upper arm. The swimmer should avoid pulling the elbows back into the ribs—a very common mistake.

PITCH OF THE HANDS

When you are in the glide position, if you were to see your hands as they are stretched outward in front of you, you would observe that they form a "V" with the palms of each facing diagonally sideward at a 45° angle and with your thumbs touching one another. That is what you would see if you are placing your hands correctly. As you begin your pull you retain this pitch (Fig. 56B), but as you pull back, your hands should change pitch gradually so that, when they start inward, the palms are facing directly backward, as in Fig. 56C. If you have an exceptionally good arm pull, we have found, you will, from this point onward, pitch your hands so they are facing diagonally backward and inward toward one another, as in Figs. 56D and 56E. This will permit you to gain some propulsion from the sculling action of the hands, even though they are not being pulled directly backward.

Your palms should never face upward during the pull or recovery.

As your hands are pushed forward into the glide position their pitch should return to the ''V'' position they held during the glide (Figs. 56H and 56I).

PRACTICING THE ARM PULL

It is good procedure for both the novice and the competitor to practice the breaststroke pull using the arms only. Such practice permits you to evaluate your pull, concentrate on its mechanics, and condition your arms. If you are a competitor, part of each day's practice should be devoted to this kind of practice. When you are practicing the arm pull, it is a good idea to use some kind of flotation support to hold your legs in the same position they assume when you are using the whole stroke. I would recommend a pull buoy or a partially inflated inner tube (as shown in Fig. 26). The correct breaststroke mechanics can also be practiced and the muscles used in performing these mechanics can be strengthened best by using the isokinetic swimming bench shown in Fig. 21.

BREATHING AND HEAD ACTION

You should breathe on every stroke when performing the breaststroke.

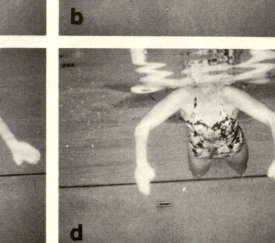

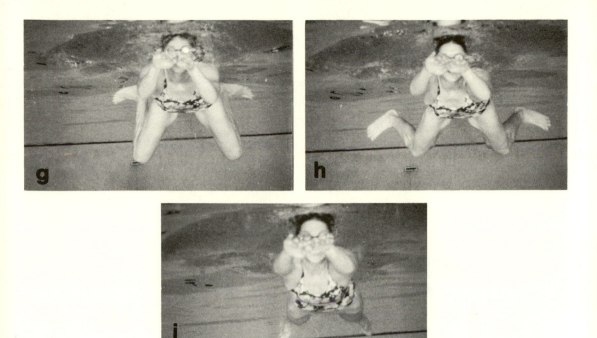

FIG. 56 *Underwater Analysis of the Breaststroke*. This sequence of pictures shows the underwater mechanics of American record holder Marcia Morey's breaststroke. It is a head-on view taken from underwater and illustrates many of the aspects of the correct mechanics of the breaststroke discussed in this chapter. Examination of these pictures should include observation of the following:

1. *Head position*. When Marcia is not lifting her head for a breath, she tilts it so she is looking diagonally downward at her hands (a). When she lifts her head for a breath, she tilts her head upward, but continues to keep her shoulders low in the water (c, d, e). This lift is accomplished by flexion and extension of the neck and prevents bobbing of the shoulders.

2. *Breathing*. The air exhalation begins slightly after the pull begins (b, c). The inhalation is made when the head is out of the water and during the last half of the arm pull (d, e).

3. *Arm pull and timing of the arms and legs*

   a & b. The pull begins with the elbows straight and the palms facing diagonally outward. The legs are fully extended.

   c. The elbows start to bend and the upper arms rotate medially as the hands press outward and backward. The hands have reached their widest spread and from this point on will move inward.

   d. The elbow bend increases as the hands are pulled inward. The hands still retain a strong sculling action on the water during this inward movement. The legs start their recovery by a slight flexion at the knees.

   e. The hands are nearing the end of the pull and are ready to thrust forward.

   f. The arms are now in the recovery phase as the knees and feet move forward in the leg recovery.

   g. The hands are thrust forward as the feet position themselves for their backward thrust.

   h. The backward thrust of the feet begins before the arms are fully extended in front of the body.

   i. The arms reach full extension as the legs near completion of the kick.

When you are not inhaling, you do not need to have your face out of
the water and you should keep it under water by flexion of your neck.
Your head should not be lowered so much that it is completely submerged. In fact, if you were a competitive swimmer, that would get
you disqualified. The amount of head movement that is desirable is
shown in Fig. 57.

FIG. 57   *Head Position and Line of Sight*
   a. Depicts the position of the head during inhalation. The bottom of the chin is in the water.
   b. The breath has already been taken; the neck has been flexed downward until the face is
slightly under water.

TIMING OF THE KICK, PULL, AND BREATHING

The breaststroke timing is somewhat more difficult to acquire than that
of the other strokes. The following description of the timing may seem
complex, but I guarantee that it is no simple procedure to explain and I
hope my attempt will not confuse you. Examination of the photographs

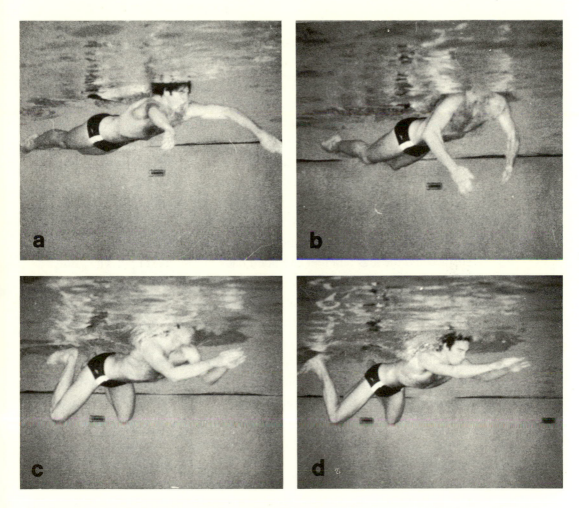

FIG. 58 *Timing of the Kick, Pull, and Breathing*

a. The pull has begun and the head is still under water, but is lifting upward and with air being exhaled. The legs remain in an extended position.

b. The pull is ending as the hands are under the shoulders. The head is completely out of the water and air is being inhaled. The legs have started their recovery.

c. The arms are moving forward in their recovery as the legs are pulled up by flexion of the hips and knees. The inhalation is complete and the face is partially under water.

d. The backward thrust of the legs begins before the arms are fully extended in front of the face. The face is completely under water with only the top of the head remaining out of the water.

should help. Figure 58 illustrates the correct timing of the stroke, as
seen from under water and from the side.

HOW LONG A GLIDE SHOULD BE USED

When you first learn to swim the breaststroke or when you swim long
distances using it, a glide should be employed after the kick and before
the next arm pull begins. You should stretch out your body with the
abdomen held in so your back is straight. Your arms should be fully
extended overhead with the hands six to eight inches below the water's
surface and the legs and feet extended back in a straight line. The glide
position can be held for a very short time, as in the case of a competitive swimmer when he is racing, or for a long period of time when you
want to swim at slow speed. The only time a glide is not used is in an
all-out sprint.

No matter at what speed you are swimming you should achieve
this fully extended glide position before the next stroke begins. Many
swimmers use the following drill to work on stroke mechanics and
body position: swim breaststroke and, holding your glide position for a

FIG. 59 (OPPOSITE) *The Long Pull after the Start and Turn*
a. After the push-off the swimmer holds the glide position for about one and a half seconds or
until he slows to swimming speed.
b. The pull begins with the palms pressing directly outward.
c. The elbows bend as the pull is made.
d. The hands come close together as the elbows continue to bend and the arms are depressed.
e. After the elbows extend, the arms are held in a position next to the body. This glide position
is held very briefly.
f. The arms are brought forward as the legs start to recover.
g. The head breaks the surface immediately after the kick begins. The swimmer will now re-
sume his surface breaststroke.

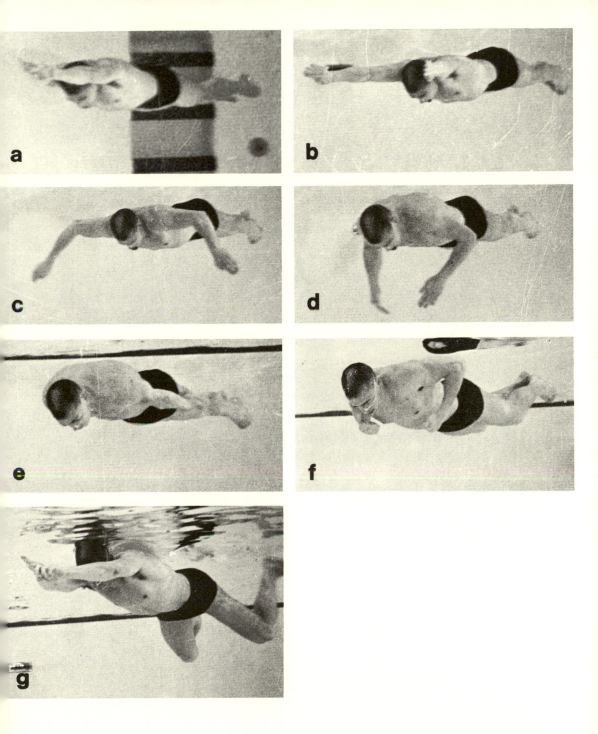

count of three to five seconds, try to swim the pool length in as few strokes as possible (five to eight strokes would be better than average in a 25-yard pool, fourteen to twenty strokes in a 50-meter pool). Try to use the technique that has been advocated in this chapter.

THE BREASTSTROKE START AND TURN

THE LONG UNDERWATER PULL AFTER THE START AND TURN

The competitive rules governing the breaststroke permit the swimmer one underwater pull and kick after the turn or start before his head must break the water's surface. A swimmer can get the most effective pull by using a long pull as shown and described in Fig. 59.

THE START

A breaststroke swimmer has a choice between the grab start and the conventional start with a circular arm swing, as described in Chapter 3 (Figs. 27 and 28). Since the breaststroke swimmer wants to dive deeper into the water than the crawl swimmer, the angle of entry should be more acute. The reason for going deeper on the start is to take advantage of the underwater stroke allowed by the rules.

THE TURN

The rules governing the breaststroke turn are similar to those for the butterfly turn. The hands must touch the wall simultaneously and on the same level and the shoulders must be horizontal. In high school and college rules the hands need not touch on the same level so long as they touch simultaneously and the shoulders do not dip. The breaststroke turn is done in the same manner as the butterfly turn (see Fig. 38).

7. The Utility Strokes

NOT ALL SWIMMING STROKES are used in competition: some are used for their utility value. Such strokes are the sidestroke and the elementary backstroke. There are a number of others: the overarm sidestroke, the inverted breaststroke, the trudgeon crawl, and so on, but they are all merely variations of the four competitive strokes, the elementary backstroke, or the sidestroke. Although the latter two strokes are slower than the competitive strokes, they can be used in lifesaving and can be swum for long distances with relatively little effort. They also are more easily learned by some people and more suitable for use by recreational swimmers who are interested in swimming at a slow cadence. They are often good lead-up strokes in preparation for learning the other strokes, but on this point I want to issue a word of caution. Since they are frequently more easily learned, you may be content to remain with them and not advance to the others. If a swimmer limits his efforts to learning only these utility strokes, he may never become a truly proficient swimmer. These strokes require less vigorous movements and do not provide the wide range of movement that involves all of the muscle groups, as do the other strokes.

I recommend that the sidestroke and elementary backstroke be learned after the front crawl, since in both of the former the swimmer can swim with his face out of the water at all times and it is better not to learn a "face out of the water" stroke first. I think you can understand that such a progression could impede or even stop progress.

Many competent swimmers who have never learned these strokes can pick them up very easily simply by reading the descriptions and looking at the diagrams, whereas the beginner may have some difficulty and have to work at these strokes just as he would at learning the others. For the beginner swimmer the elementary backstroke should be introduced into the practice sessions immediately after learning the front crawl. The sidestroke can follow the elementary backstroke and then the beginning swimmer may go on to the remaining strokes: breaststroke, back crawl stroke, and the butterfly, in that order.

THE BACK FLOAT

This skill has some value as a lead-up to learning the correct body position for both the elementary and the back crawl strokes. I have already mentioned that only a few swimmers can float in a horizontal position on their backs in fresh water, although most people can accomplish this skill easily in salt water. Most people can, however, float on their backs in a vertical hanging position. Read the following instructions carefully and try this method of floating.

You will find it desirable to practice this skill in a calm pool. Get close to the side of the pool and place your body against the wall with your entire front surface touching the wall. Extend your arms sideward with your elbows straight, as in a swan dive, and bend your knees 90°. Grasp the top edge of the pool gutter with your thumbs, keeping the rest of your hands and arms under water. Keep your body low in the water by submerging your shoulders and neck. Without pulling your chest away from the side of the pool look directly upward and extend your neck backward so your face is in the horizontal plane (Fig. 60A). Place as much of your head under water as you can without submerging your mouth and nose. At this point every part of your body except your thumbs and part of your face (your breathing apparatus) is under water.

Now inhale as much air as you can by breathing in through your mouth until you think your lungs are full. The big tendency at this point is to tense the rib cage and take in only a small gulp of air. Let me emphasize that you should take a deep inhalation lasting several seconds. The breathing action should involve so much action of the diaphragm muscle that you feel the abdominal area pushed outward. Remember that the additional inhalation of only a couple more cubic inches of air may be the difference between floating and not floating.

If you feel yourself starting to sink, lift your chin higher and gently tilt your head back. This action will submerge more of your head and this may be enough to keep you floating.

Remember to keep your arms submerged and at the side, as in a swan dive. If your legs start to rise to the surface, your arms can be raised slowly overhead, always keeping them under water. To achieve a more horizontal position, bend at the hips as if to pull the knees closer to the surface, as shown in Fig. 60C.

FIG. 60   *The Back Float*

Few people succeed in mastering this skill the first few times they try, but by getting the details clearly in mind and by repeating the skill over and over, you will join the more than 95 percent of all people who can float in this manner.

It is important to remember to hold your breath during this float, for if you exhale even a small amount there is a tendency to begin to sink. You should hold your breath until your position has become stabilized—this may take ten to fifteen seconds—and when you do breathe, you should exhale a small amount of air and immediately inhale again. Your entire exhalation/inhalation should take less than a second. You should then hold your breath again for a five- to ten-second period and repeat the same breathing action.

THE ELEMENTARY BACKSTROKE

The back float position described above is a good preliminary skill to learning the proper body position for the elementary backstroke and the back crawl.

BODY POSITION
Lie in the water on your back, looking directly overhead with your head tilted back enough so your ears are in the water (Fig. 62A).

Your chest should be near the surface of the water with your body as close to a horizontal position as possible. Unless you are progressing forward you may find your legs dropping, since this horizontal position can be held by only a small percentage of swimmers who are very buoyant. If, however, you have pushed off the side or bottom of the pool in a horizontal position on your back, you will be able to maintain this position for a short period of time, that is, until you begin swimming. One of the factors in maintaining a streamlined horizontal position is the forward speed of the body through the water. The resistance created on the underside of the body causes it to plane and to stay near the surface. If you glide too long between each stroke, however, you may find your feet starting to sink.

THE INVERTED BREASTSTROKE KICK
The inverted breaststroke or frog kick is used in the elementary

backstroke. In Chapter 4 and Fig. 50 this kick is described and shown in detail, so I won't repeat it here.

The inverted breaststroke kick should be practiced on land before it is tried in water. The swimmer should sit on the pool edge, leaning his trunk backward and resting on his forearms, while allowing his heels to touch the water (as in Fig. 9). He should then practice the kick in three counts.

Count 1. Pull the heels up toward the edge of the pool by bending the hips and knees (Fig. 62C). Keep the heels close together and spread the knees slightly.

Count 2. Spread the feet apart and dorsiflex the ankles (Fig. 62D).

Count 3. Thrust the legs backward and squeeze the feet together (Figs. 62E, 62F, 62G).

Once you believe you have mastered the movement with your eyes closed, try it in the water while holding on to the edge of the pool. This can be done in pools that have a low, flat overflow gutter by placing the back of the head on the gutter and grasping the gutter with the hands placed directly over the shoulders, palms down. Pull against the gutter with your hands and your feet should rise upward. People who find this drill too difficult or who do not have the right type of overflow gutter available can practice the breaststroke kick by holding on to the gutter in the manner suggested when practicing the crawl flutter kick (Fig. 10), that is, while lying in the water on your chest. One hand should be placed down about a foot and a half below the surface and the top hand should grasp the gutter directly over the other hand. Pull with the top hand and push with the bottom hand. This will cause the feet to rise to the surface. It is extremely important that the swimmer who is learning or has a poor breaststroke kick do these drills frequently.

It is also important that the swimmer understand the necessity for pushing the water backward with the soles of his feet, if his kick is to be effective. In the fishtail and flutter kicks the propulsive force is derived from pushing the water with the tops of the feet. Thus, the feet must be extended (plantar flexed) or even hyperextended to be effective. But in the breaststroke or inverted breaststroke kick the feet must be flexed (dorsiflexed) to be effective. Figures 52 and 53 illustrate two drills that can be used to develop the necessary ankle flexibility for a good breaststroke kick.

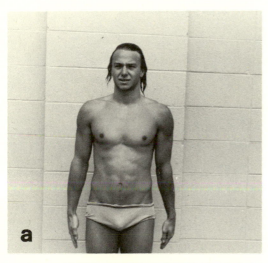

FIG. 61   *The Elementary Backstroke Arm Action*
    a. Standing erect with your arms at your sides.
    b. On the first count, bring your hands up to your shoulders, but keep your elbows at your sides.
    c. On the second count, extend your arms diagonally overhead in a V position with the palms facing outward. On the third count, keeping your elbows straight, pull your arms downward in a sweeping motion to your sides, which is the original starting position (a).

THE ARM ACTION

In performing the arm action of the elementary backstroke the arms move simultaneously and identically. Figure 61 shows a dry-land drill that you can use to familiarize yourself with this movement.

COORDINATION OF THE ARMS AND LEGS

The timing of the arms and legs in the elementary backstroke is beautifully simple. The arm and leg recovery is made simultaneously and so is the arm pull and leg kick. Figure 62 pictures the mechanics of the elementary backstroke as seen from underwater.

THE INVERTED BREASTSTROKE

At this point you might like to try a variation of the elementary backstroke which some people find to be more suitable for them. In this stroke variation the timing of the arms and legs changes, so the propulsive phase of the kick and the arms is alternated.

The starting position for the stroke is with the arms extended directly overhead instead of at the sides, as in the elementary backstroke. After the pull the arms are pushed overhead in a line directly over the shoulders, not diagonally outward as in the elementary backstroke. As they are extended overhead the backward thrust of the legs is made and a slight glide is held before the arm pull is repeated.

Occasionally I swim a few lengths of this stroke in my workouts just to test the efficiency of my breaststroke kick and to add some variety to my workouts. I recommend that you try both the elementary backstroke and the variation just described.

THE SIDE STROKE

The sidestroke is a good resting stroke. Although it was a competitive stroke seventy-five years ago, it is now used primarily for its utility value since its mastery is necessary for certain lifesaving techniques, such as the level-off, the cross-chest carry, and so on.

Figure 64 is an underwater view of the sidestroke and Fig. 63 illustrates and describes a dry-land drill that will familiarize you with the stroke mechanics and coordination.

BODY POSITION

As the name implies, the sidestroke is swum while the body is lying in a horizontal side position with one side of the head resting in the water with the neck turned slightly upward in order to maintain the mouth clear of the water. As in all strokes, the swimmer should try to keep his body in a flat, streamlined position.

THE KICK

The scissors kick is used with the sidestroke. When lying on the side one leg is moved forward and the other leg is reached backward as if you were taking a long stride (Fig. 63C and Figs. 64F and 64G). The legs are then squeezed together (Fig. 63D and Figs. 64G and 64H).

Before practicing the scissors kick in the water, you should do the dry-land drill shown in Fig. 63, then try the kick from a stationary position while hanging on to the edge of the pool.

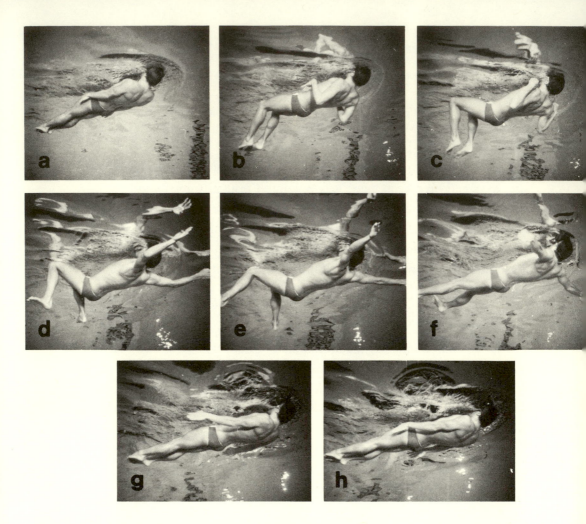

FIG. 62   *A Sequence of Pictures Showing the Coordination of the Arms and Legs in the Elementary Backstroke*

a. The body is fully extended with the hands at the sides and the head laid back so the ears are in the water.

b. The arms and legs start their recovery phase.

c. The elbows reach maximum bend as the hands pass by the shoulders. The knees and hips continue to flex.

d. The hands are pushed overhead in a **V** position as the feet position themselves to push backward.

e. The backward thrust of the feet and the pull of the arms begin simultaneously.

f. The legs squeeze together as the arms sweep downward toward the hips.

g. The kick finishes before the arm pull is completed.

h. The kick and the arm pull are now complete and the swimmer holds the glide position momentarily before beginning another stroke.

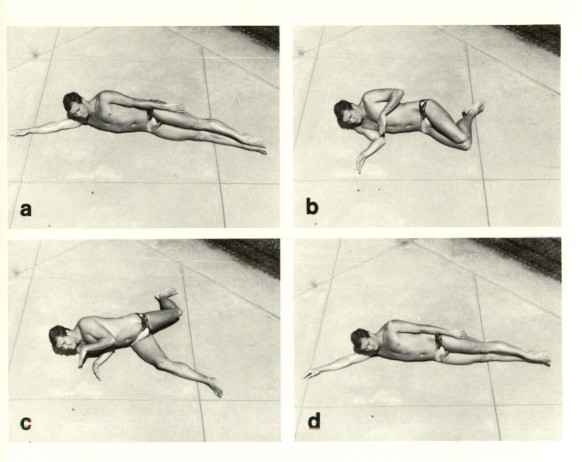

FIG. 63 *Dry-Land Drill for Learning the Sidestroke*

a. Lying on your side with your legs fully extended, extend the bottom arm forward and over-head and hold the top arm at the side.

b. On the first count, bring the heels up toward the hips and lift the top hand toward the chest, while pulling the bottom hand down.

c. On the second count, spread the legs as shown and continue the upward movement of the top hand and the downward movement of the bottom hand until they pass one another.

d. On the count of three, squeeze the legs together and reach out with the top hand and pull down with a sweeping motion until the hand returns to the starting position. At the same time push the bottom hand forward. Hold this position for a short glide. When the top leg moves for-ward in the manner just described, it is referred to as a normal scissors kick; when it moves backward, it is called an inverted scissors kick. Both are acceptable.

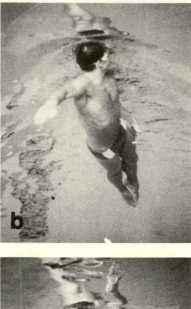

FIG. 64 *The Sidestroke As Seen from under Water*

    a. Pictured is the starting or glide position. The bottom arm is fully extended forward. The legs are held completely extended.

    b. The bottom arm is pressed downward as the top arm begins moving upward.

    c. The bottom arm bends at the elbow as the hand presses firmly against the water. The legs start to recover by bending at the hips and knees.

    d. The bottom arm has finished its pull as it nearly touches the top arm. The legs continue to recover.

    e. The bottom arm has finished its pull and is being pushed forward into its recovery phase; the top arm is beginning its pull. The legs continue to spread in their recovery phase.

    f. The top hand presses backward with the wrist flexed. The legs are ready to begin the scissors (squeezing) phase, which is the propulsive part of the kick.

    g. The bottom arm is pushed forward into an almost fully extended position as the leg squeeze begins.

    h. The top arm finishes its final push as the legs finish the kick and as the bottom arm becomes fully extended overhead. The swimmer will now assume the glide position shown in (a) and will hold this position for a short pause before beginning another stroke cycle.

FIG. 65 *Scissors Kick Drill.* Hanging on to the side of the pool with the top hand holding the pool gutter edge and the bottom hand braced against the wall two feet below the surface, directly under the top hand, pull with the top hand and push against the wall with the bottom hand. This will cause the body to rise to the surface. Practice the kick in the water as it is shown in the dry-land drill.

8. Training

THE IMPROVEMENT IN competitive swimming times over the past thirty years has been due primarily to improvements in training methods. Today many thirteen-year-old boys and girls swim faster than former Olympic champions Johnny Weissmuller and Buster Crabbe did at the peak of their careers. Most of the swimmers of Johnny and Buster's era and the period preceding it used two methods of training, while most of today's competitive swimmers combine four methods of training into a complete program.

The two earliest methods of training used were overdistance training and sprint training. If you had watched a swimmer train during Johnny and Buster's years (1920s and 1930s), you would have seen him do a workout something like this:

1. Swim one mile (1760 yards) continuously at a slow-to-moderate speed.

2. Kick a half mile (880 yards) on a kickboard at moderate speed.

3. Pull a half mile (880 yards) with a tube wrapped around the

legs, or a kickboard held between the legs, or some other form of flotation device being used to keep the legs at the surface.

4. Swim two all-out 50-yard sprints, followed by two all-out 25-yard sprints.

While this is not a bad workout and might be used today by some competitive swimmers in early season, it is neither long enough nor sufficiently intense to condition today's competitive swimmer for to-day's high level of performance. The average high-performance swimmer—in both the age-group and senior divisions—today trains between 5000 and 12,000 yards a day, with a few swimmers training as far as 15,000 yards a day during the peak of training.

The present-day swimmer not only trains a greater distance, but also uses two methods of training that yesterday's swimmers had never defined and were only vaguely aware of. These two methods are called interval training and repetition training.

Before proceeding with a description or definition of these methods, it might be more enlightening for you if I review some of the principles of training and show how they are implemented by the training methods.

The terms "training," "conditioning," and "getting into shape" are used frequently by athletes. While there is a general understanding of these terms, most people—even the athletes—don't know spe-cifically what happens to the athlete who trains and "gets into shape."

First, there is the concept of adaptation. The human body is a very adaptable organism that has the important trait of being able to change itself when a stress is placed on it so as to better handle this particular stress. The classic example of this ability to adapt is the practice of immunization—the stress being the introduction of weakened or killed bacteria and the adaptation being the production of antibodies. Stress takes many forms and so do the adaptations our bodies make. In the case of athletics, when an athlete says he is "getting into shape," he means his body is adapting to the stress of the conditioning program. His body changes in many ways to better accommodate the stress of exercise. His heart becomes more efficient because it can pump more blood; his lungs increase in size and efficiency and he is able to absorb more oxygen into his blood. This oxygen is carried to his muscles by the blood and, as a result of the increased heart and lung efficiency, his endurance is improved. This type of endurance is referred to as cardiorespiratory endurance (heart-lung) and is best improved by training long-distance or by using a method of training known as *interval training*.

Although I am sure you know this, the above adaptations happen to you as well as to champion athletes. In fact, this is one of the primary reasons why you should learn to swim and then use your new skill to improve your physical condition.

THE FOUR METHODS OF TRAINING

There are essentially four methods of training for swimming at this time. Although all four have been mentioned before, below you will find them listed again, this time with the purpose of describing them and mentioning what quality or qualities they develop.

OVERDISTANCE TRAINING

The title is self-explanatory. You swim a certain distance, 800 yards for example, that is greater than the distance you will swim in the race for which you are training. Of course, you must swim this distance at a speed slower than you will swim in a race. There are several ways you can swim overdistance:

Without timing. This method is not highly motivating for most people. Unless you are being timed or are timing yourself, you tend to swim too easily and fail to place sufficient stress on your body to bring about the desired physiological changes that result in good conditioning. If, however, you are extremely tired and feel that hard swimming would make you even more tired, you can swim this method without pushing yourself too hard.

Out slow—back faster. This method of swimming overdistance is challenging to most swimmers and is used by such great swimmers as Gary Hall, Mark Spitz, John Kinsella, and Shane Gould. You swim the first half of the overdistance swim at a slow or moderate pace, then you pick up the tempo and swim the second half faster. Thus, if you are swimming an 800-yard overdistance swim, you swim the first 400 yards in 5 minutes, taking a look at the pace clock as you turn at the halfway point, then pick up the pace and swim the second 400 yards in 4 minutes and 40 seconds for a total elapsed time of 9 minutes, 40 seconds (9:40.0).

Holding a steady pace. Most swimmers seem to prefer doing most of their overdistance swimming at a steady pace. If you are swimming 800 yards and want to swim it in 9 minutes and 20 seconds (9:20.0), each 100 yards will have to be accomplished in 1 minute and 10 seconds (1:10.0). As you complete each 100 yards, you should glance at the pace clock to see if you are swimming on pace.

Speed play. A method of overdistance training that is borrowed from track and that is sometimes used by swimmers is called Fartlek training, which, literally translated from Swedish, means "speed play." You swim an overdistance, such as 2000 yards, or a specific time period, such as one hour, and during that time you vary your speed from slow to moderate to fast. You can even time certain segments of the total distance on a pace clock if you desire. I often use this method in my practices for Masters swimming. Here is an example of this type of workout: swim for one half hour, and at some point in this period, using a pace clock, time 2 x 200, 4 x 100, and 4 x 50. To introduce you to swimmers' parlance: 2 x 200 means two efforts of 200 yards or meters each, 4 x 100 means four efforts of 100 yards or meters each, and so on. I will use this means of communicating numbers of efforts (also called repeats or repeat efforts) and the distance throughout this chapter and the chapters covering the organization of practice (Chapter 9) and workouts (Chapter 10).

Back to speed play. In the time between these various swims, you swim continuously at a slow pace.

Overdistance interval training. It is possible and even desirable to swim a set of overdistance swims in the interval training method. For example, three times 800-yard swims with 30 seconds rest between each effort (3 x 800 with 30 secs. R.I.). You are challenged more and can swim at a faster pace than if you just swim the same distance of 2400 yards continuously.

Pulse rate during overdistance swimming. The pulse rate will vary in overdistance swimming, depending on how much effort you expend. If you are swimming 2000 yards and timing it to get your best time ever, toward the end of your race your pulse rate may approach as high a level as you can push it at any time—180 to 200 beats per minute. Ordinarily, however, it will be a good deal less than that on the average, being between 130 to 150. I will often stop one or more of my university swimmers when they are swimming overdistance and take their pulse rate. If it is not at least 130, I tell them they are not working hard enough and they should increase the amount of effort.

Qualities built by overdistance swimming. Overdistance training is used principally to improve cardiorespiratory endurance. The heart and lungs become more efficient, with the result that more oxygen is available and more carbon dioxide can be removed from the muscles. Within the muscle, at the cellular level, the muscle fibers develop more myoglobin, which permits them to carry on aerobic work more efficiently. There is also an increase in the number of mitochondria and a consequent enhancement in the endurance level of the muscle. More functional capillaries are opened and many subtle adaptations are made by the body which enable it to better handle the stress the next time it is imposed. Your body can easily absorb a large volume of overdistance training without becoming exhausted; it cannot handle large amounts of high-quality work such as is encountered in sprinting or repetition training.

It is an important concept to remember that the heart is conditioned by keeping the pulse rate elevated for relatively long periods of time. When a swimmer swims 1500 meters with a continuous elevation of the heart rate to a high level, such as between 130 and 180 beats per minute, he is doing much to improve the efficiency of his heart.

Two Types of Training Using Intermittent Work

A major part of the training of swimmers involves some form of intermittent work. Intermittent work consists of swimming, kicking, or pulling a given distance and then taking a controlled interval of rest before repeating the effort and rest sequence, sometimes as often as forty or more repetitions. Training using intermittent work comprises two methods, each of which is sufficiently distinct from the other to be classified separately. They are *interval training* and *repetition training*.

Interval training. In the late 1940s interval training was introduced into the competitive swim program. The term derives from the fact that the swimmer performs a series of repeat swims and controls the interval of rest. For example, he may swim 10 x 100 repeat swims with 15 seconds' rest between each 100.

When using either form of intermittent work—interval training or repetition training—the swimmer must determine four factors:

    1. What the distance of his swims will be,

    2. The number of repeat swims he will perform,

3. What the interval of rest between each repeat swim will be,* and

4. How fast he will swim each repeat or, in other words, how much effort he will exert in each swim.

I believe it is important for you to know not only "what to do" but "why you are doing it." Therefore, I will give you a brief explanation of how to answer these four questions.

1. First, you should usually swim your repeat swims at the same distance for which you are training or at under that distance. If you are training for the 100- and 200-yard distances, you should swim your repeat swims at any or all of these distances: 200 yards, 150 yards, 100 yards, 75 yards, or 50 yards. A general rule to remember is that the longer the distance you swim in each repeat, the more you are building endurance and the less emphasis you are placing on speed. The reverse is also true: the shorter the distance you swim in your repeat swims, the greater emphasis you are placing on building speed and the less you are placing on endurance. Since you want to build both qualities, when training for a given distance, say 200 yards, you should sometimes swim your repeats at 50 yards, sometimes at 200 yards, and sometimes at a distance in between. Varying the distance swum also provides variety in the workouts and keeps your interest from lagging.

2. You can best learn from experience how many repeats you

---

*The interval of rest between each repeat swim is controlled by most swimmers by using departure times rather than by controlling the exact interval of rest. If a swimmer is swimming 10 x 100-yard repeat swims with a rest interval of 30 seconds and he swims each 100 in exactly 60 seconds, he will start a 100 repeat swim every minute and a half. This time is referred to as the departure time (D.P.). The problem with using an exact interval of rest such as 15 seconds is that the mathematics become confusing to the swimmer. If he swims the first 100 in 58 seconds, he must then depart on 1:28; if the next 100 repeat is done in 1:03, he then must depart on 1:33 seconds, and so on. The reader will see references to both rest interval and departure time in this book. Since the various members of a team will swim their repeat efforts at different speeds, in order to have approximately the same amount of rest, there will have to be at least several different departure times.

should swim. There are certain guidelines that most of today's competitive swimmers stay within: approximately 40 to 70 percent of the total workout should be swum in repeat swims of one form or another.

3. A good principle to follow in determining the interval of rest is this: the shorter the period of rest, the more emphasis is being placed on building endurance. If only 5 to 10 seconds is permitted between each repeat, you have too little time for your pulse rate to drop significantly and you can recover only part of your oxygen debt. After a repeat swim, your pulse rate might be at 160 to 180; in such a short interval of rest as 5 or 10 seconds your pulse rate will only drop to between 130 to 160. This means your repeat swims will be slower than if you allowed a longer rest period and a greater recovery of the heart.

4. The speed at which the swimmer swims his repeat swims is determined largely by the previous three factors. The shorter the distance, the fewer the number of repeats, and the longer the rest period, the faster he should try to go and vice versa. A more detailed method of determining the speed at which the swimmer should swim his series efforts will be discussed later in this chapter.

Below are listed the times achieved by John Kinsella, former world record holder at 1500 meters freestyle, while doing various sets of 100-yard repeat swims. John's best 100-yard freestyle time is :46.1.

	Rest Interval	Average Time	Av. Pulse Rate after Repeat	Av. Pulse Rate before Repeat
A. 30 x 100 yds. freestyle	5 secs. D.P. 60 secs.	:55.2	174	163
B. 10 x 100 yds. freestyle	40 secs. D.P. 1:30 secs.	:50.4	181	124
C. 4 x 100 yds. freestyle	5 mins. d.p. 6 mins.	:48.2	184	88

A. This type of training would qualify as short rest interval training and would be used principally to improve endurance.

B. This medium rest type of training introduces more speed than did A, but retains some elements of endurance training, since the heart rate remains elevated until the next repeat is begun.

C. This long rest interval type of training is referred to by some coaches and athletes as merely another form of interval training. Many people, including me, believe there is a sufficient difference between this type of training and that of the short rest interval type of training that it should be classified differently. We call this high-quality, long-rest type of intermittent work *repetition training*.

Repetition training. When doing repetition training the swimmer is allowed sufficient rest for his heart rate to return close to normal—at least under 100. His efforts are made at almost maximum effort and he is working anaerobically (without oxygen) through much of the swim. That is, he works so hard that he is not able to replenish his oxygen supply as he swims. The result is that he finishes in oxygen debt and is short of wind with a lot of respiratory difficulty. He literally pants after the effort is completed. This specific stress is due to the oxygen debt that he has built up and is the stress that brings on some desirable adaptations of the body that will improve his ability to swim sprints and middle distances at an intense speed. It is a different type of stress than he encounters when he swims distance or short rest interval training and, consequently, brings about different kinds of physiological changes.

These changes permit the body to become more efficient in the quick-energy release that is required for this intense type of work. The

FIG. 66   *The Pace Clock*

respiratory muscles become stronger, the heart becomes capable of sustaining a greater pumping capacity. At the cellular level such changes occur as an increase in the number of mitochondria. The *law of specificity* comes into effect. That is, the body makes specific adaptations to specific stresses. Since this type of training more closely simulates the type of stress a swimmer will encounter when swimming the 100-, 200-, and 400-meter races, it is important that all swimmers, including sprinters, middle distance, and distance swimmers, use this type of training.

Too much use of high-quality, long-rest repetition training can cause you to become excessively tired. It must be used sparingly, perhaps only two or three times a week. Low-quality repeat swims such as are done in the interval training method can be used more frequently without the risk of exhausting the swimmer. When swimmers speak of lower quality, they mean the repeats are slower relative to their faster efforts. Everything is relative to this kind of training. If you add one stressful factor, such as higher speed, you must remove another, such as short rest. If you make the rest short, you must reduce speed. If you didn't, you would become *too* tired. One of your important obligations in training is not to get so tired that your body can't recover by the next day's training.

Determining the speed of swim series, when using interval or repetition training. The speed you should go on each swim depends to a great extent on the elements mentioned in the discussion earlier: the length of the interval of rest, the number of repeat swims being swum, and the total number of repeats you are going to do. There is no formula that can be set down, such as if the swimmer swims an all-out 50-yard freestyle in 23 seconds, when he swims 30 x 50 with a departure time of 60 seconds, he should swim all of his 50s 20 percent slower than his best time, or in 27.6 seconds. We know from experience that there are so many individual differences that the application of any formula is impossible. Each person can best learn from experience what he should do for the various sets of repeats. If you are doing 20 x 50 with a departure time of 60 seconds, by doing them once and then repeating them again in a few days or a week and by trying to improve your average time, you soon learn to what limits you can or want to extend yourself. After you have done the same set several times, a pattern will emerge that will include a peak time at which you will level off. Once you have learned to pace your efforts and to push yourself hard through the entire set and obtained what you feel is your best average time, you are only capable of improving this time by improving either your conditioning or your stroke efficiency, or both. This is one of the real challenges and satisfactions in swimming—to see your practice times improve. Because you are then assured of an improvement in your race times. Many swimmers keep a logbook in which they carefully record all of their practice times. They can tell you their best set of repeats for 20 x 100 or 10 x 200 and so on. At a typical meeting of swimmers after practice, a conversation might go like this:

"Did you hear what Gary went for 10 x 150 fly?"

"Yes, I heard he averaged 1:26.5, he ought to be able to get the American record now."

"How about John's 500s, he averaged 4:38." And so on.

If you are interested in becoming a swimmer or a coach, you must learn to memorize these average times and to know their significance. Let me emphasize that there is no exact manner by which a swimmer's repeat times can be precisely predicted. Your times will even vary from one day to the next. As mentioned previously, the best way to determine what times you should be accomplishing is through your experience.

SPRINT TRAINING

Some sprint training can be integrated into nearly every practice session, once the height of the training season is reached. The sprinter, of course, should do more sprint training in his workouts than the distance swimmer. However, it is important for the distance swimmer to do some sprint training because he will need some speed when he moves down to swim the 200-yard distance, which is now getting to be an extended sprint event.

Sprinting places a different stress on the body than do the other methods of training. Because the muscles are working against greater resistance encountered at the higher speeds, they adapt by becoming stronger. The athlete also trains his neuromuscular system to coordinate his movements at these faster speeds. A swimmer who does nothing but slow, easy swimming in his training will feel uncoordinated when he tries to sprint.

INTEGRATING THE FOUR METHODS OF TRAINING INTO ONE WORKOUT

No single kind of training is a complete method of training. You should plan to use three and sometimes even all four in one workout. This integration or mixing of the various methods into one workout has two purposes: to permit variety and prevent boredom and to place different kinds of stress on your body in order to develop both speed and endurance. Table 1 illustrates an integrated workout used by the members of the Indiana University swimming team at the height of the indoor training season. The table also lists the qualities that each type of training develops and the physiological changes that are made as a result of this type of training.

TABLE 1

INTEGRATING THE FOUR METHODS OF TRAINING
INTO ONE WORKOUT

Workout Item	Type of Training	Quality Developed and Physiological Adaptations
1. Warm up 800 yds.	Overdistance Training	The warm-up is done at an easy pace, its purpose being to stretch out the muscles, route the blood flow to the active muscles, and prepare the body for the harder efforts which will follow.
2. Swim 8 x 200 yds. with 15 secs. rest intervals (Total: 1600 yds.)	Short Rest Interval Training	This type of training is primarily used to develop endurance. Endurance is improved by increasing cardiorespiratory efficiency and changing the muscles themselves at the cellular level. These changes include increases in the number of functional capillaries and in the number of mitochondria in each active muscle fiber.
3. Swim 800 yds. for time—negative splitting	Overdistance Training	Same quality of endurance as listed above under (2).
4. Kick 800 yds. continuously at a moderate speed	Overdistance Training	Same as under (2), but the fact that less blood flow is directed to the arms allows the muscles of the legs to be stressed more than when the total stroke is used.

5.	Kick 8 x 25-yd. sprints with 30 secs. rest interval (Total: 200 yds.)	Sprint Training	Develops speed in the kicking muscles. The muscles become stronger and the neuromuscular system develops the ability to coordinate kicking movements at fast speed.
6.	Pull 6 x 150 yds. with 30 secs. rest interval (Total: 900 yds.)	Interval Training	Affects endurance favorably because of the same factors mentioned under (2) above.
7.	Swim 4 x 100 yds. with 5 min. rest interval	Repetition Training	Anaerobic capacity (the ability to work at intense levels for moderate periods of time) is improved. There is a change in the muscles at the cellular level. The enzymes affecting the rate of metabolism are altered favorably. The heart becomes capable of maintaining a high output for a longer period of time.
8.	Swim 4 x 25 yds. from a dive at all-out speed with a 2 to 3 min. rest interval	Sprint Training	The muscles become stronger—the same result as were listed under (5) above.

Total yardage: 5600

CHANGING EMPHASIS AS THE SEASON ADVANCES

Early in the season, emphasis in the training program should be placed on the types of training that develop endurance (overdistance and short rest interval training) with only a small degree of emphasis being placed on the types of training that develop speed (sprint training and repetition training). As the season progresses the amount of speed work should be increased, but with a constant awareness of what has been said in this chapter about excessive use of the training techniques that develop speed but tend to tire the swimmer too much and tend to result in poorer performances.

THE TAPERING PERIOD

In preparing for the big meet, such as the NCAA Championships or the Olympic Games, the swimmers use a period of reduced work in order to rest for a maximum performance. It is normal procedure for outstanding swimmers to train right through the rest of the year's competition. That is, they rest very little or not at all for less important meets in order that they may not miss many days of training. On the day of a dual meet many of the swimmers at Indiana University will take a normal workout before the meet, swim in the meet, and take another workout after the meet. They realize that if they miss too much work for any reason, whether it is illness or a routine competition, they risk getting out of shape or, at best, not improving conditioning. Therefore, they use a "taper" only once or twice a season, when they want to perform their best efforts.

The tapering period usually lasts two to three weeks and, while the amount of work done in terms of total yardage will decrease, it is important to remember that it must not be reduced so much that you begin to lose conditioning. While you can count on the fact that it is necessary to reduce the total yardage, there are no formulas or percentage drop-offs that you can use to arrive at the best taper for every individual. Tapering seems to be an individual matter. Here are a few guidelines within which to work in fashioning your taper.

1. Gradually decrease the total distance done daily without radically changing the pattern of your workouts. How many times have I heard the laments of the well-trained swimmer who tried to increase the amount of speed work during this period and who got overtired. While a little more speed work should be introduced into the first part of the tapering period, watch carefully about overdoing it. Do not eliminate overdistance completely or short rest interval training, since they are not hard on you and will keep your endurance high without fatiguing you.

A typical reduction in work for a group of college swimmers who normally train a total of 10,000 to 12,000 yards per day in two workouts per day might be as follows:

First three days of taper—Reduce to a total of 7000 to 8000 yards daily

Second three days of taper—Reduce to a total of 6000 to 7000 yards daily

Third three days of taper—Reduce to a total of 5000 to 6000 yards daily

Fourth three days of taper—Reduce to a total of 4000 to 5000 yards daily

Last three days before meet—Reduce to a total of 1500 to 3000 yards daily

2. The last three days of the taper should be devoted to easy swimming and kicking with some emphasis on short sprints and some pace work. If you are not in shape going into the last three days, you cannot improve your conditioning during this period without getting tired, so avoid heavy work during this final period.

3. Be sensitive to the way you are feeling during the taper period. Do not follow a preplanned program of taper if your body tells you that you are too tired. On the other hand, if you are feeling too rested and want to work a little harder because you think you are getting out of shape, do so. It is better, however, to be a bit too rested than to be a bit too tired.

A further discussion of "tapering" will be included in the chapter containing sample workouts (Chapter 10). The amount of warm-up before a race will also be discussed there.

9. The Organization of Practice

AT THE PRESENT TIME the training of swimmers is much more formal and controlled than it was in the past. Swimmers and coaches use stopwatches or, even better, pace clocks with a sweep second hand to measure and control not only the speed at which they swim, kick, or pull and the interval of rest between repeats, but also their heart rate. It is almost impossible to do the type of training that is used today without a pace clock. It has become almost as indispensable as the swimming pool. Some of these clocks are large—four feet square—and can be seen from any place in the pool by all the members of the team; others are small—one foot square—and can be placed before a lane and can be clearly seen only from a few feet away. If you are the only swimmer training and have to take a clock with you each day to the pool, I recommend that you look for such a small, portable clock with a sweep second hand as I have described above. They can be found in some discount or department stores for under thirty dollars.

Some are battery-run and some are spring-operated. I have also been informed by the manufacturer of the large pace clock pictured in Fig. 66 that his company is in the process of producing a small battery-operated clock for individual use. You can expect to see it advertised in the swimming and track publications within a few months of the release of this book.

USE OF THE PACE CLOCK IN TRAINING

When first using the pace clock, you may become slightly confused. A first reading of this discussion will probably not clear things up. A pace clock cannot be used efficiently in a matter of days or even weeks; its intelligent use comes with practice and involves a high degree of concentration along with a good memory. Even now, after using a pace clock for many years as a swimmer and as a coach, I sometimes forget in my workouts whether I began my last 50 when the sweep hand was on 0, 5, or 10 on a repeat swim.

When using a pace clock either for one person or for an entire team, it is important to understand that the pace clock should not be started and stopped at any time during the practice, but should be kept running continuously. The reason is easy to figure out if you give it a little thought. When a team is training, in order that each member may be able to look at the clock and get his time when he finishes his repeat swim or his rest interval, the clock has to be kept in operation. Before the use of the pace clock was introduced, the coach spent most of his time running back and forth with his stopwatch, trying to keep repeat times for each person. The concept of interval training is largely based on controlling repeat times and rest intervals, so the coach often found himself spending each training session in this timing process. After the advent of the pace clock, the coaches who tried to start and stop the clock were in exactly the same situation as before—the advantage of the device was lost.

The clock is also left running even when only one person is using it and the reason for this will become obvious too as you read the following section.

THE USE OF DEPARTURE TIME RATHER THAN A CONTROLLED INTERVAL OF REST

If you have set up a workout of 10 x 50-yard repeats with 30 seconds rest and you swim the first 50 in 32 seconds and you are using a pace clock that runs continuously, you will have to start your next repeat 50 when the second hand is on 2. If you swim the second 50 in 32.5 seconds, you will have to start the third 50 on 4.5 seconds. It becomes clear that soon the mathematics of this process will become so complex that your mind is boggled in trying to decipher exactly what you are doing. Most swimmers and coaches, therefore, have learned to do their repeats on a departure time. For example, instead of doing 10 x 50 with 30 seconds rest, you would do 10 x 50 on a departure time of 60 seconds. Every time the second hand hit 0, you would start another 50. You would also be able to keep track of your average time more easily and would be bothered less with mathematics. The use of departure time instead of interval of rest is a necessity in a team practice in which many swimmers are swimming circles in one lane.

There is a method of training called broken swimming, which will be discussed later, in which the exact interval of rest is held constant. I will not discuss this kind of swimming at this point since it will only confuse you.

If you are not familiar with the use of the pace clock, I would recommend that you find a clock with a sweep hand and practice a few drills.

DRILL 1

Imagine you are swimming 5 x 100 on a departure time of 1:30 and your average time for swimming the 100 is 1:08. Assuming you will start your first 100 when the second hand is on 0, where will the second hand be when you finish the first 100? Where will the second hand be when you start the second 100? The third? Etc.

DRILL 2

You are going to swim 6 x 50 on a departure time of 45 seconds and your average time will be 35 seconds. You start your first 50 when the sweep second hand is on 0. Complete the following chart.

	Starts on	Finishes on
1st 50	0	35
2nd 50	45	20
3rd 50		
4th 50		
5th 50		
6th 50		

DRILL 3

You are swimming 4 x 200-yard swims (8 lengths of a 25-yard pool) on 2½ minutes departure time and your average time will be 2:10 per 200-yard repeat. Oh yes, *and* you are swimming in a lane with five other swimmers. You are the third swimmer and you are allowing 5 seconds departure time between each swimmer. The first swimmer leaves when the sweep second hand is on 0, the second swimmer leaves when the hand is on 5, and you leave on 10. Complete the following chart.

	Starts on	Finishes on
1st 200	10	20
2nd 200	40	
3rd 200		
4th 200		

HOW TO TAKE PULSE RATE AND ITS USE IN TRAINING

Whether you are six or sixty, your pulse rate serves as an important

FIG. 67 *Circle Swimming*. The swimmers in Lane 1—closest to the pace clocks—are training in a circle pattern in a counterclockwise direction. Each swimmer swims down the right side of the lane. After he turns, in order to avoid bumping into the swimmer in back of him, he pushes off to the other side of the lane and continues to swim on the right-hand side of the lane. If a swimmer overtakes the swimmer in front of him and wants to pass, the overtaken swimmer moves closer to the right side of the lane and the swimmer who wants to pass moves toward the center of the lane or to the left of the swimmer he is overtaking.

The swimmers in Lane 2 are swimming in a circle pattern in a clockwise direction. This plan makes allowance for the possibility of bumping a swimmer in the next lane or hitting him with a recovering arm by assuring that the swimmers next to the lane markers will be going in the same direction. The swimmers in Lane 3 (not shown) will swim in a counterclockwise direction, the swimmers in Lane 4 will go in a clockwise direction, etc.

guide in any training program. Therefore, it is necessary to understand a few principles concerning pulse rate before its use can be applied intelligently. The pulse rate indicates how fast your heart is beating and usually is expressed in terms of beats per minute. The average resting pulse rate varies with a person's age, level of conditioning, and, like every other human trait, such as height and weight, etc., varies considerably from one individual to the next.

The number most frequently given as normal resting pulse rate for a young man in his late teens is 72. If he were to get into good physical condition, this rate would be somewhat lower and, if he were to get badly out of condition, it would be higher. If he were to become extremely fatigued or ill, it would rise. It would also rise if he drank a cup of coffee or ate a large meal.

I mention these things in order that you may understand how variable the resting pulse rate can be and you may not consider it to be a constant thing in an individual. While training will cause a slight decrease in resting pulse rate and many well-trained athletes, particularly distance swimmers, have resting pulse rates in the low 50s or even high 40s, our main concern in training is not with the resting pulse rate, but with the pulse rate during and after exercise. Without the use of electronic equipment, it is difficult to impossible to take the pulse rate of a swimmer during the time he is swimming. As soon as he stops, however, the coach or the swimmer can check his heart rate easily. If you are taking your own pulse rate, as soon as you finish your effort (swim, kick, or pull) you should stand on the bottom of the pool or hang on to the edge of the pool with one hand and take your pulse rate with the other hand, as shown in Fig. 68. Do this by looking at the pace clock and counting the number of beats for six seconds and then multiplying by 10 or by counting the beats for ten seconds and multiplying by 6. Never take it for any period longer than ten seconds

FIG. 68   *Taking Pulse Rate*
    a. Place the index or middle finger on the carotid artery on the neck and under the jaw.
    b. Place the hand on the chest under the breast and slightly to the left.

because your pulse rate begins to drop immediately after the exercise stops. If you take it for too long a period after exercise finishes, you will actually be measuring it after it has dropped somewhat.

The elevation of pulse rate is an indication of how much effort you have expended in that particular part of your workout. The higher the pulse rate, the greater the effort. After a 100 percent—or all-out—effort for 200 yards, you will have a pulse rate of 180 to 200 beats per minute regardless of your resting pulse rate. After a very easy 200-yard swim of, say, 50 percent effort, your pulse rate might be elevated to a level of only 110 beats per minute.

As indicated in the discussion of resting pulse rate, variation from one individual to the next is considerable and variation from day to day in the same individual is also probable.

You can use the pulse rate as a diagnostic tool in helping you set up your practice sessions, for it determines how much effort you are putting into each phase of your workout. As you become more knowledgeable, you can often combine the times you are swimming on various repeat swims with your pulse rate to determine whether you are really tired and should slacken off or whether you are just feeling lazy and are not putting out enough effort.

For example, let us say that you would normally swim 10 x 100 on a departure time of 1:10 and average 60 seconds per 100 with a pulse rate after each repeat of 150. On a particular day you are doing the same routine, but you are averaging 65 seconds instead of your usual 60. You are not sure whether you have a case of the blahs and are not particularly motivated that day or whether you are really tired and need a little rest. You take your pulse rate and, if it is elevated to 150 or more, you know you are trying as hard as usual, but are tired or coming down with an illness—perhaps a cold. If, on the other hand, your pulse rate is only 110, you know there is probably nothing wrong with you physically and that you are just being lazy and not putting forth enough effort.

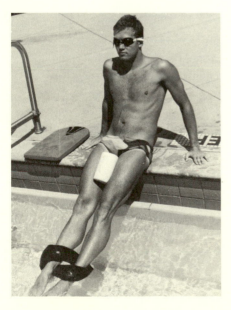

Fig. 69 *Swimming Workout Equipment*. The swimmer is wearing goggles. They protect his eyes from the irritation caused by the presence of chlorine and other chemicals in the pool water. The kickboard lying next to him is used for kicking drills. The pull buoy between his legs and the pulling tube wrapped around his ankles are the choices he has for use in pulling drills. He will choose one of the two or may even use both simultaneously.

THE NEED FOR WELL-ORGANIZED
PRACTICE SESSIONS

Practices should start on time and be well organized. The athletes are
expected to put in a lot of effort during practice. The coaches and team
managers should also work hard not only during practice but in preparation for it. The lane markers and backstroke turning flags should be
put in place before practice starts. Equipment such as pace clocks,
kickboards, pulling tubes—or pull buoys—should be placed in the
immediate area of the pool where they will be easily available to the
swimmer. Figure 69 shows some of this workout equipment.

The coach should not only conduct well-organized workouts, he
should plan them carefully. There should be an overall plan of training
and the athletes should be made aware of this plan. A weekly meeting
is a must; a short daily meeting sometimes helps pull things together.

The coach must let the swimmers know what is expected of them
in practice. Many coaches post the workout on a chalkboard (Fig. 70).
Others may prefer to explain to the swimmers what they are going to
do in the next part of their training routine only after they have finished
the preceding part. Either system is satisfactory as long as the athletes
have confidence that the coach is running a well-planned, well-
organized, and efficient practice session.

IG. 70   *Practice Routine Posted on a Chalkboard*

10. Training Routines

WHEN SWIMMERS AND COACHES get together, the main topic of conversation is the workout routines they have been doing or they have heard someone else has been doing. There are almost as many varieties of workout as there are swimming teams. Each swimmer thinks, or hopes, his workouts are better than those of the swimmer he is competing against.

The type of workout a swimmer does depends on many factors, including time available in the pool, the number of swimmers training with him, the amount of energy he can afford to expend on swimming—because of school work or other factors—and so on. For these reasons it behooves every swimmer to use his time in the pool intelligently in order to get the most from the time available to him. That is what I want to help you do as well.

There are only four elements you can combine into a practice, although the combinations are practically endless:

1. Swimming sets of repeats in one of the following methods:
   A. Interval training
   B. Sprint training
   C. Repetition training
2. Swimming overdistance
3. Kicking—which can be done in any of the four methods named above
4. Pulling—which can also be done using interval, sprint, or repetition training or using overdistance.

These elements can be arranged in any sequence desired. The most common plans or formats are listed below, with sample distances and sets also provided:

FORMAT A

1. Warm-up overdistance—800 yards
2. Swim a set of repeats in interval training method—15 x 100 with about 10 to 30 seconds rest
3. Kick a total of 800 yards in one training method or another
4. Pull a total of 800 yards
5. Swim a set of long rest interval training or repetition training repeats—6 x 200 with 3 minutes rest
6. Swim a set of sprint repeats—8 x 25 with 30 seconds rest
Total distance—5300 yards
Total time allowed—1:45 to 2 hours

FORMAT B

1. Warm-up 200 swim, 200 kick, 200 pull, 200 swim
2. Kick 8 x 100, using short rest interval training
3. Pull 8 x 100, using short rest interval training

4. Swim one long set of interval training repeats—8 x 400 with 30 seconds rest or less

5. Swim one set of sprint repeats—4 x 50 with long rest, 1 minute rest or more

Total distance—5800 yards

Total time allowed—1:45 to 2 hours

It is possible to build a case for any format of workout. It is even a good idea to change the format of your workout occasionally to give variety to your workouts. Doing so also gives you an opportunity to try different plans in an effort to find the format you prefer. But—a note of caution in regard to placing the sprints in your workout plan. If you sprint early in the workout, you may become somewhat tired and the rest of your workout may suffer. If, however, your sprinting is always done at the end of the workout, you may never get accustomed to swimming fast except after several thousand yards of swimming, kicking, and pulling. That is, you may not be able to sprint fast in a race without a very long warm-up. Don't laugh, I have seen many swimmers in just such a predicament. I would, therefore, recommend that the sprints usually be placed near the end of the workout as listed in the two formats above, but that occasionally you do them early in the workout to simulate the precise conditions you will encounter in a meet. On that day—say, once a week—I also recommend that you start with the exact warm-up you will use in competition.

Establishing Warm-up Procedure

The purpose of the warm-up before a race is to stretch out the muscles, get the "feel" and timing of your stroke, and get the body ready for exertion. Each swimmer must determine the amount of warm-up that is best for him and the amount you will need is something you determine through trial and error—the learning process that you know by now I believe in. In the workout below I list a typical warm-up that could be used by a good age-group swimmer, a high school swimmer, or even a college swimmer.

FORMAT C

1. Warm up just as you would the day of a competition
   A. Swim 400 easy to loosen up
   B. Kick 200 easy
   C. Swim 4 to 6 x 50 on 60 seconds, beginning at a moderate pace of 60% effort and increasing until the last 50s are at 85% effort
   D. Kick 2 or 3 x 50 at 60% to 75% effort
   E. Swim 2 to 4 x 25—beginning at 80% effort and swimming the last at 100% or maximum effort

2. On the day of your competition you are now ready for your race. At this point in your workout, you might want to try to swim a time trial or do a set of high-quality repeats. Choose from either of the following:
   A. Time an all-out 150 yards swim *or*
   B. Swim a set of 8 x 50 on 1:30 departure time—90% to 95% effort

3. Kick 400 easy, then kick 8 x 50 on departure time of 1 minute

4. Pull 400 easy, then pull 400 for time

5. Swim 6 x 300 with 30 seconds to 1 minute rest

Total distance—4500 to 4800 yards
Total time allowed—1:45 to 2 hours

WORKOUTS FOR AGE-GROUP SWIMMERS

Age-group swimming should be explained before proceeding. It is a

phenomenon that began over twenty years ago and has grown to en-
compass all states in the Union and many countries abroad and includes probably over a half million children and teen-agers at any
given time in the United States. In the following section I am talking
about children from about six to seventeen years of age.

Many of our age-groupers in their early teens, in particular the
girls, are among the best swimmers in the world and train as hard as
any college or senior swimmer. This type of swimmer would not want
to use any of the workouts listed in this section. The workouts for
national-caliber swimmers will be described later in the chapter. Those
presented here are for the age-group swimmer who is still early in his
or her career and only wants to—or can only—train about an hour
daily.

Workouts for 1500 to 3000 yards a day—1 to 1:15 hours

FORMAT A
   1. Warm-up 200-yard swim
   2. Swim 4 x 100 on departure time of 2 or 2½ minutes
   3. Swim 200 yards continuously
   4. Kick 200 yards, then 2 x 50
   5. Pull 200 yards, then 2 x 50
   6. Swim 6 x 50 on departure time of 1 or 1½ minutes
   Total distance—1500 yards
   Total time allowed—1 hour
FORMAT B
   1. Warm-up 200-yard swim
   2. Swim 10 x 50 on departure time of 1 to 1½ minutes
   3. Kick 200 yards, then 6 x 25
   4. Pull 200 yards, then 3 x 50
   5. Swim 4 x 200 on departure time of 4 to 5 minutes
   Total distance—2100 yards

Total time allowed—1 hour

FORMAT C

    1. Warm-up 400-yard swim

    2. Swim 6 x 75 on departure time of 1½ minutes

    3. Pace 400—out slow, back hard

    4. Kick 200 easy, then 2 x 100 hard

    5. Pull 200 easy, then 2 x 100 hard

    6. Swim 300, rest 30 seconds to 1 minute, then swim a 200, rest 30 seconds to 1 minute, then swim a 100, rest 30 seconds to 1 minute, then swim a 50

Total distance—2600 yards

Total time allowed—1:10 hours

FORMAT D

    1. Warm-up 400-yard swim

    2. Swim 5 x 100 on departure time of 1½ to 2 minutes

    3. Kick 100 easy, then 6 x 50 hard

    4. Pull 100 easy, then 3 x 100 hard

    5. Swim 3 x 400 with 1 to 2 minutes rest interval

    6. Swim 4 x 25 sprints

Total distance—3000 yards

Total time allowed—1:15 hours

Workouts for 3500 to 5000 yards a day—1 hour, 30 minutes to 2 hours.

If the workouts listed above are too easy for you and you are finished easily within the time allotted, increase the distance you swim in each section of the workout. Below are listed some of the workouts of a longer and more intense nature.

FORMAT A

    1. Warm-up 400-yard swim

    2. Swim 16 x 50 on departure time of 1 minute or less

3. Swim a moderate 400 for time, 75% effort

4. Kick 5 x 100 on departure time of 2 minutes

5. Pull 5 x 100 on departure time of 2 minutes

6. Swim a moderate-to-hard 400, 80% effort, making certain you go harder than you did in (3) above

7. Swim 3 x 200

8. Swim 4 x 25 sprints

Total distance—3500 yards

Total time allowed—1½ hours or less

FORMAT B

1. Warm-up 200 swim, 200 kick, 200 pull

2. Swim 6 x 100 on departure time of 1½ to 2 minutes, 8 x 50 on departure time of 50 seconds to 1 minute

3. Pull 400, then 8 x 25 on departure time of 30 seconds

4. Kick 200, then 4 x 50 on departure time of 1 minute

5. Swim 800 for time, 80% to 90% effort

6. Swim 4 x 200 on departure time of 3 to 4 minutes

7. Swim 8 x 25—every other one at maximum effort, others easy

Total distance—4000 yards

Total time allowed—1½ hours

FORMAT C

1. Warm-up 200 swim, 200 kick, 200 pull, 200 swim

2. Swim 8 x 150 yards on departure time of 2 to 2½ minutes

3. Swim 10 x 25 yards, sprinting at 95% effort

4. Pull 200 yards easy, then 3 x 200 yards at 85% effort

5. Kick 200 yards easy, then 6 x 100 yards on departure time of 2 minutes

6. Swim 2 x 400, 2 x 100, 2 x 50, 2 x 25

Total distance—5000 yards

Total time allowed—2 hours or less

WORKOUTS FOR HIGH SCHOOL, COLLEGE, AND SENIOR SWIMMERS

At the present time, world-ranked swimmers swim between 8000 and 15,000 yards daily. Some of them train twice a day with one short workout and one long one; while others who work out twice a day split their workouts evenly, doing approximately the same distance in each workout. Which system is best? No one can tell you definitely, although several probably have definite opinions. Oh yes, this is a seven-day-a-week schedule, with an occasional person taking off a full day—usually Sunday—but most swimmers taking off only a half day.

The pattern that has been established by most swimmers in the United States varies with the time of the year. During the indoor season, when the swimmers are attending school, the shortest workout is almost always in the morning and lasts about 1 to 1½ hours. It takes place before classes, while the long workout (2 to 2½ hours) is in the afternoon, after classes. This arrangement is often reversed in the outdoor or summer season, in which swimmers do their longer workout during the morning due to the availability of the pool.

In the case of Mark Spitz, when he was attending Indiana University and class was in session, he attended morning workouts from about 7:00 to 8:00 (an hour to an hour and a half), during which time he swam 3000 to 3500 yards. The longer workout was in the afternoon and lasted two to two and a half hours (from 3:45 to about 6:00), during which time he trained a distance of 7000 to 7500 yards. Sometimes, once or twice a week, Mark would miss morning practice, but would attend late-evening practice from 9:00 to 10:00, during which he concentrated on sprints and swam only a total distance of 1200 to 2000 yards.

In the summer, when he was not in school, this procedure was reversed and Mark trained 7000 to 8000 meters in the morning in a workout of two and a half hours. In the afternoon he swam a total distance of 3500 to 4000 meters in a workout of an hour and a half.

The ensuing part of this section will be devoted to a description of the training procedures and actual workouts of some champion swimmers. In some cases their tapering method and warm-up procedure will be included. Whether you are a beginning competitive swimmer training only 3000 yards a day or a world-ranked swimmer training as much as 15,000 yards a day, you may gain something from studying these workouts. Before beginning the actual workouts, it might be well to present the framework within which these workouts must be organized.

THE INDOOR SEASON

In the United States there are two competitive swimming seasons. The indoor season begins in November or early December and ends with the National AAU Championships in early April. Most of the competition during this period is held in short-course pools, either 25 yards or 25 meters long. The NCAA (National Collegiate) Championships are normally held in the last weekend of March. Most high school state championships take place during the months of February and March, although there is a wide variation in scheduling, with California, some other western states, and Florida holding their championships in April or May, and some states, such as Washington, having theirs as early as January.

Because of the difference in scheduling there are many differences in the time at which each swimmer wants to peak for his best performance of the season and this causes some variations in program. Other factors affect training patterns: the level at which the swimmer is competing and the section of the country he is from cause important differences. However, most swimmers of national caliber try to swim their very best times in late March and early April, at the end of the indoor season, and the year's training program outlined in Table 2 is planned with this in mind.

THE OUTDOOR SEASON

The outdoor season usually begins in late May or early June and culminates in the National Junior Olympic Championships and the National AAU Championships in late August. The outdoor competition is normally held in long-course—50-meter—pools.

To compete on the national level it has become important—almost necessary—to train during both seasons. Some swimmers will take a two-, three-, or even four-week break between seasons; others take no break at all and train twelve months of the year. I believe that a short break in training between seasons is needed to rest both the body and the mind, but I realize that there are individual differences in personality, in levels of motivation, and in tolerance to withstand physical and mental stress. For this reason, within limitations, I give the swimmers on my team some leeway in what they do between seasons. Below is outlined the year-round program of a former world record holder in the 100-meter freestyle, Jim Montgomery, an Indiana University swimmer. Jim is primarily a sprinter and also holds the American record for the 200-yard freestyle. He also won the World Championship in the 200-meter freestyle event, as well as the 100-meter distance.

TABLE 2

Jim Montgomery's Training Program for One Year

Month	Dry-Land Exercise	Number of Pool Workouts per Week	Total Distance Covered Each Day (yds.)	General Description of the Types of Training Used
		Indoor Season		
September	Primarily done on Mini-Gym swim bench 3–5 times a week, ½ hr. each	No formal workouts in the pool	o	
October	Five times a week, 45 mins.–1 hr. each	5	4000	Overdistance, short rest interval training, and a few sprints
November	Five times a week, 45 mins.–1 hr. each	1st week: 6 2nd week: 7 3rd week: 8 4th week: 9	A.M. workouts 4000 P.M. workouts 7000 to 8000	Overdistance, short rest interval training with emphasis on developing more speed in the various repeat swims
December 1–15	Five times a week, 1 hr. each	10	A.M. workouts 4000 P.M. workouts 7000 to 8000	During the Christmas holiday Jim trains very hard since there are no class commitments. The team usually goes to Hawaii or Florida to train in a long-course pool
December 15–31	No dry-land exercise during this period	13	A.M. workouts 7000 to 8000	

			P.M. workouts 5000 to 6000	
January and February	Five times a week. ½ hr. each	11	A.M. workouts 4000 P.M. workouts 8000	As the season progresses more emphasis is placed on speed work. More repetition and sprint training is introduced into the training program
March	Three to four times a week only, 15 mins. each	9	A.M. workouts 2000 to 3000 P.M. workouts 3000 to 5000	Jim reduces training in order to rest (tapering). Work is gradually reduced until he is going only 3000 yds. a day. The NCAAs are the last of March and he aims to peak for this meet
April	Five times a week, 45 mins. each	5 to none		The season is completed with the National AAUs in early April. Jim will take a 2- to 3-week break. He will continue work on the isokinetic exerciser

May and June	Five times a week, 45 mins. each	9 to 12	A.M. workouts 7000 to 8000 P.M. workouts 4000 to 5000	Jim starts back in the water following the 2- to 3-week break. Since the outdoor season is short, hard training must start immediately with a program combining the three training methods. 1st week, 9 workouts; 2nd week, 10; 3rd week, 11; 4th week, 12
July	Five times a week, 30 mins. each	9 to 12	A.M. workouts 6000 to 8000 P.M. workouts 2000 to 3000	During July there are some important meets at which Jim wants to swim fast. He may rest a few days by decreasing the distance of each practice or even miss a session.
August	No dry-land exercise	7 to 10	A.M. workouts 3000 to 4000 P.M. workouts 2000 to 3000	This month culminates in the National AAU Championships, the meet to peak for. Three weeks prior Jim begins his taper by reducing his work in order to rest

Dry-Land Exercise

Dry-land exercises are used to strengthen the muscles that the swimmer uses to pull him through the water. A swimmer should not engage in a general strengthening program that will cause him to acquire extra bulk which he will then have to pull through the water. The primary muscles he should develop are the arm muscles that are used in the pull and the leg muscles that are used in the push-off, the start, and the kick.

Most world-class swimmers in the United States do as Jim Montgomery does and perform their exercises on an isokinetic exerciser called the Mini-Gym. The Mini-Gym isokinetic exerciser is arranged in different pieces of equipment in such a manner that the muscles may be exercised precisely as they are used when swimming, diving for the start, or pushing off. For more information about this equipment write Dr. James E. Counsilman, Indiana University Athletic Department, Bloomington, Indiana 47401.

SAMPLE WORKOUTS OF CHAMPIONS

Jim Montgomery

Early Season—November

A.M. 1. Warm-up 600
2. Swim 10 x 125, departure time of 1:30
3. Kick 300, then 2 x 125
4. Pull 300, then 2 x 125
5. Swim 3 x 250 on 3 minutes
Total distance—3700 yards

P.M. 1. Warm-up 800 (200 swim, 200 kick, 200 pull, 200 swim)

2. Swim 5 x 200 on 2:30
   5 x 200 on 2:15
3. Kick 400
4. Kick 6 x 100 on 1:40
5. Pull 1000 continuously
6. Swim 5 x 400 on 4:30
7. Swim 8 x 25 sprint with 1 minute rest interval
   Total distance—7000 yards

MID-SEASON—JANUARY

A.M.   1. Warm-up 600
2. Swim 20 x 50 on 40 seconds
3. Kick 8 x 50
4. Pull 8 x 50
5. Swim 400, 300, 200, 100, 50
   Total distance—3450 yards

P.M.   1. Warm-up 800
2. Swim 10 x 100 on 1:10
   5 x 100 on 1:05
   5 x 100 on 1:00
3. Swim 12 x 25-yard sprints, every other one all-out, the others very easy, departure time 30 seconds
4. Swim 800—first 400 in 4:10
   second 400 under 4 minutes
5. Kick 300 easy
6. Kick 14 x 50, departure time 50 seconds
7. Pull 300 easy
8. Pull 7 x 100, departure time 1:15
9. Swim 4 x 300 on 3:10
10. Swim 2 x 50 sprint from a dive

Total distance—7200 yards

END OF SEASON—TAPERING PERIOD (MARCH)

A.M.   1. Warm-up 400

2. Swim 3 x 150

   3 x 100

3. Kick 400

4. Kick 2 x 50

5. Pull 400

6. Pull 2 x 50

7. Swim 12 x 50, every other one fast

   Total distance—2750 yards

P.M.   1. Warm-up 800

2. Swim 3 broken 200s—4 x 50 with 10-second rest interval, descending times

3. Kick 400

4. Kick 1 broken 200—4 x 50 with 10-second rest interval

5. Pull 400

6. Kick 1 broken 100—4 x 50 with 10-second rest interval

7. Swim 4 x 25 sprints, 1-minute rest interval

8. Swim 1 x 100 at 85% speed—in a time of 48 seconds or better

   Total distance—2700 yards

Jim Montgomery's Warm-up

Jim arrives at the pool one hour before the beginning of the meet.

1. Swim 400 to 800 yards or meters—easy swimming and some kicking

2. Swim 2 to 4 x 50—starting off with a moderate effort of 75% and ending up with a last 90% effort

3. Loosen down with 100-yard easy swim
4. Swim 2 x 25-yard or meter sprints from a dive for time
5. Loosen down with 100-yard easy swim

John Naber
MID-SEASON—FEBRUARY

A.M.   1. Swim 2000
Mon.   2. Kick 1000
       3. Pull 2 x 800
         Total distance—4600 yards

P.M.   1. Swim 1500
Mon.   2. Kick 3 x 200, 100, 50
       3. Swim 10 x 150 Back on 2 minutes
       4. Swim 3 x 500 Free on 6 minutes
       5. Swim 5 x 500 Free on 4 minutes
       6. Swim 7 x 100 Back on 1:30
       7. Kick 500
       8. Swim 10 x 50 sprint on 1:30
         Total distance—8750 yards

A.M.   1. Swim 3300
Tues.   2. Kick 4 x 175 on 15 seconds
       3. Pull 500
         Total distance—4500 yards

P.M.   1. Swim 2000
Tues.   2. Swim 4 x 200 Free on 2:20
       3. Swim 5 x 300 Free on 3:15
       4. Swim 20 x 200
       5. Kick 500
       6. Swim 4 x 50 sprints on 1:30

Total distance—9000 yards

A.M.   1. Swim 500, 400, 300, 200, 100 on 30 seconds

Wed.   2. Kick-swim 2 x 500

       3. Swim 1, kick 1, pull 1—3 x 800

         Total distance—4900 yards

P.M.   1. Swim 800

Wed.   2. Kick 10 x 100 on 1:45

       3. Pull 6 x 400 on 5 minutes

       4. Swim 1000, 800, 500, 400, 300, 200, 100 on 30 seconds rest

       5. Swim 4 x 400 on 2 strokes and 5 minutes

         Total distance—9100 yards

The following workout is typical of one that John Naber would use during the summer season, probably in June.

A.M.   1. Warm-up 800

Long   2. Kick 400

Course   3. Pull 400

       4. Swim 4 x 800 (2 are Back, 2 are Individual Medley)

       5. Pull 15 x 100 with paddles

       6. Kick 8 to 10 x 100

       7. Swim 10 x 50 sprints

       8. Swim 1 x 200 easy

         Total distance—7800 meters

         Time allowed—2 hours

P.M.   1. Warm-up 1 x 400 swim

Short   1 x 200 kick

Course   10 x 50 working on stroke

       2. Swim 4 to 5 x 100 descending each time, 10 to 20 seconds

rest after each one, working on individual strokes
3. Kick 5 x 250 descending series
4. Swim 10 x 25, departure time 20 seconds
    8 x 25, departure time 18 seconds
    6 x 25, departure time 16 seconds
    4 x 25, departure time 15 seconds
    1 x 1000 working on turns
    Total distance—6450 yards

David Willkie

David is primarily a breaststroke swimmer, having won world titles and swum in two Olympic Games. He has also held the world record in the individual medley. The following are typical workouts for the indoor season.

EARLY SEASON—OCTOBER (5 workouts per week)
1. A. Swim 500 I.M.
    B. Pull 500 Back
    C. Pull 12 x 75 on 1:15 (3 of each stroke)
    D. Swim 500 easy
    E. 15 minutes of dry-land exercise
    F. Swim 3 x 500 on 6:15
    G. Swim 48 x 12½ on 20 seconds—no breath
       Total distance—4500 yards

2. A. Swim 400 Free, 300 Back, 300 Breast, 300 Free-Fly meters
    B. Kick 500 meters
    C. Swim 4 x 50 underwater on 1:30, 3 breaths
    D. Swim 4 x 400 Free, negative split on 7:30
    E. Swim 600, stroke drills
    F. Swim 4 x 200 negative split Breast on 4
       Total distance—5000 meters

NOVEMBER–DECEMBER (7 workouts per week)
  Mon.–Fri. Afternoons (Short Course)
  Tues. and Thurs. Mornings (Long Course)

3. A. Swim 1000, change strokes
    B. Kick 500
    C. Kick 3 x 200 on 3:30
    D. Kick 2 x 100 on 1:50
    E. Kick 8 x 25 on 30 seconds
    F. Swim 16 x 25 underwater on 35
    G. Swim 5 x 200 broken on 4, 10 seconds rest at 50s
    H. Swim 1000, work turns hard
    I. Pull 5 x 100 on 1:30
    J. Pull 5 x 100 on 1:25
    K. Swim 5 x 100 on 1:20
    L. Swim 5 x 100 on 1:15
        Total distance—6900 yards

4. A. Swim 100 Fly, 200 Back, 150 Breast, 200 Free, 500 Fly, 300
        Back, 350 Breast, 400 Free
    B. Kick 600, slow/fast
    C. Kick 8 x 100 on 1:45
    D. Pull 800 Breast
    E. Swim 200 on 3 ⎫
              100 on 1:30 ⎬ Five times through with no rest
              2 x 50 on 1 ⎭
        Total distance—6000 yards

MID-SEASON—JANUARY AND FEBRUARY (10 workouts per week)
5. *A.M.* (Long Course)
    A. Swim 700

    B. Kick 10 x 50 on 1

    C. Swim 5 x 200 I.M. reverse on 3:15

    D. Swim 6 x 200 on 3

    E. Swim 10 x 100 on 1:40 slow/fast

    F. 2 x 50 for time

       Total distance—5000 meters

6. *P.M.*(Short Course)

    A. Swim 4 x 375 on 5:30

    B. Swim 5 x 125 on 2:15

    C. Pull 5 x 175 Breast on 3:30

    D. Swim 10 x 25 on 30, no breath

    E. Swim 9 x 50 Free on 40

    F. Kick 5 x 400 on 6:30

    G. Swim down 300

       Total distance—6000 meters

LATE SEASON—MARCH (Short Course)

(Typical workout ten days before NCAAs)

7. A. Swim 4 x 100 on 1:30 descend

    B. 6 x 50 on 1 descend

    C. Swim 100

    D. Swim 4 x 50 Breast on 1 descend

    E. Swim 1 x 200 Breast, broken with 10 seconds rest at 50s
       (all-out with 3 pulse checks every 30 seconds after finish)

    F. Swim 100

    G. Swim 3 x 200 Free, negative split on 3:15

    H. Swim down 100

       Total distance—2000 yards

Shirley Babashoff

    Shirley, an Olympic champion freestyler, is a middle-distance swimmer, holding the world record for the 400-meter freestyle and the American record for the 200-meter event.

MID-SEASON (Long Course)

A.M.   1. Warm-up 400

2. Swim locomotive to 4 and back down

1 length fast   1 length easy

2 lengths fast   2 lengths easy

3 lengths fast   3 lengths easy

4 lengths fast   4 lengths easy

3. Pull 6 x 200 on 3 minutes, descended 1 to 3

4. Kick 10 x 50 Free, on 1 minute

5. Swim 20 x 100—10 on 1:15, 1 to 5

5 on 1:12, 1 to 5

5 on 1:10, 1 to 5

6. Swim 4 x 50 sprints, 1 of each stroke on 1 minute 1 to 4

7. Swim 400 easy

P.M.   1. Dry-land exercise—½ hour*

2. Swim 20 x 50 on 50—warm-up

3. Pull 4 x 400 on 6, 1 to 4

4. Kick 3 x 100 of each stroke on 2:10, 1 to 3

5. Swim 8 x 250 I.M. (100 Fly, 50 Back, 50 Breast, 50 Free)

6. Swim 10 x 50 on 50 seconds, breathing every 7 strokes, descended 1 to 5

7. 10 x 50 on 45 seconds, breathing every 5 strokes, descended 1 to 5

8. 10 x 50 on 40 seconds, breathing every 3 strokes, descended 1 to 5

9. Swim down 400

*Shirley uses isokinetic exercises as part of her dry-land program.

TAPER—LATE SEASON
A.M.   1. Swim 1000
2. Pull 8 x 100 on 1:40
3. Kick 8 x 100 on 1:15
4. Swim 6 x 200, descended on 3:20
5. Swim 3 x 50 of each stroke on watch
6. Swim 300 easy

P.M.   1. Swim 500
2. Kick 500
3. Pull 500
4. Swim 20 x 50 on 40 seconds, descended 1 to 4
5. Swim 3 x 400 1 easy
1 broken, 10 seconds, at 100
1 broken, 10 seconds, at 50
Descended
6. Swim 4 x 50 sprint on watch
7. Swim 400 easy

Camille Wright

Camille is a butterflier and has won national championships at the 100- and 200-meter distances.

A.M.   1. Warm-up 400
2. 15 x 100 Fly (100 pull on 1:30, 100 kick on 2:00, 100 swim on 1:30)—repeat
3. 15 x 100 Free (100 pull on 1:20, 100 kick on 2:00, 100 swim on 1:20)—repeat
4. Swim 40 x 15 sprints, every 30 seconds

P.M.   1. Swim 400 warm-up

2. Kick 10 x 50 on 60 seconds
3. Pull 10 x 50 free style on 45 seconds
4. Pull 3000 alternative one length free and one length butterfly
5. Swim 20 x 50 using all strokes on 60 seconds
6. Swim 10 x 100 individual medley on 2 minutes.

11. Competitive Swimming— Its Organization

THROUGHOUT THIS BOOK I have from time to time mentioned world-class swimmers and swimming. I have done so despite my intention to keep with my main subject—learning to swim. I suppose it is only natural that a coach of competitive swimming would begin to think of getting his students into a race as soon as he has them swimming well. I think there is another factor as well: people of all ages enjoy rating themselves against others to see how their skill or performance ranks and there will probably be a number of readers of this book who will want to do likewise. This chapter will inform them of the structure of the competitive swimming organization, both national and international. It will not be detailed, but will provide the necessary names and addresses where more detailed information can be obtained.

In the United States the governing body for all amateur sports is the Amateur Athletic Union (AAU). The exceptions are the interscholastic and intercollegiate bodies which control high and prep school, college and university sports respectively. FINA* is the governing body for international aquatic competition, including that of the Olympic Games.

The National AAU headquarters is located at 3400 West 86th Street, Indianapolis, Indiana 46268. It is from there that you can obtain rule books and all information pertaining to national competition. On a local level the national body has established fifty-eight district associations, each usually comprising a state, although in some highly populated areas there may be more than one district in a state. An example is Pennsylvania: the upper western part is in the Lake Erie Association along with the upper eastern section of Ohio; the western third is in the Allegheny Association; and the eastern section is in the Mid-Atlantic Association along with portions of some other states.

Thirteen regions have also been designated, each encompassing several associations. The regions are fairly recent divisions which were formed because of the growth in interest in competitive swimming. They permit regional competition in amateur sports, but play a relatively minor role in their administration.

Each district association controls the sanctioning of meets, the registration of athletes, and the membership of clubs within the district. Each association administers its district within the framework of the national organization. Every amateur sport controlled by the AAU has representation in the association in which it is located and every association sends delegates to the annual national convention.

Three programs have evolved in competitive swimming: (1) the Age-Group Program, (2) the Senior Program, and (3) the Masters Program.

*Fédération Internationale de Natation Amateur.

THE AGE-GROUP PROGRAM

This program has been divided into five age divisions which conform roughly to the maturation process of children. The divisions are: 8 and under, 9–10, 11–12, 13–14, 15–17. When a swimmer reaches age eighteen, he *must* compete as a senior, although he may begin at age twelve.

THE SENIOR PROGRAM

After a swimmer has completed the age-group program, or when he is younger if he can meet the time standards, he may want to compete in senior swimming. Both men and women can find competition at the district, regional, and national levels. Years ago, when I swam in the senior program, there were so few competitive swimmers that no time standards were required even for the national championships. Now a swimmer must meet stringent cut-off times (standards) to be eligible to enter national competition and sometimes even regional and local meets. This is because there are so many swimmers who would like to compete in these meets that their numbers must be reduced to keep these meets from becoming unwieldy and lasting all day—and all night too—for each day of a three-day meet.

Many districts have this problem as well and have had to solve it by instituting time standards or by holding preliminary meets. Except in lightly populated areas where swimmers have to travel long distances to find competition, most swimmers can find scheduled meets in sufficient numbers and within reasonable distances to keep their interest stimulated and their experience assured.

THE MASTERS PROGRAM

Masters swimming has entered the picture only recently. Now

that people are aware of the need for a regular exercise program in their lives, competitive swimming for older people (twenty-five and older) was destined to evolve from swimming for fitness. Many people have adopted swimming on a regular basis to fill the need for exercise. They could swim alone and without competition and derive the same physical benefits, but the competitive aspect provides social bonding opportunities and satisfies the urge of many people to test their accomplishments against those of their peers.

I believe it also keeps people swimming who might otherwise slacken off or stop completely. Although it is true that the program contains many former senior competitors, there are a good number who only learned to swim during adulthood and are now competing for the first time. Swimming is an ideal fitness activity for "mature" adults. It is a non-weight-bearing activity which makes it ideal for people with joint problems who have had to stop jogging. It is a more complete exercise than many other activities because it conditions the heart and lungs so well. Any person who embarks on this program would be well advised to be checked by a doctor before beginning. I think most people have heard of cases in which swimming was recommended by a doctor as a means of regaining good fitness levels, so I don't hesitate to recommend it. As I stated in the introduction of this book, I now train for Masters swimming. When I began I was fifty pounds heavier than I am now, and I led a stressful life as the coach of a nationally prominent team. In short, I was the classic candidate for a heart problem at the age of forty-eight. Now, at fifty-five, I look and feel better, I have made good friends who share my interest in Masters swimming, and I enjoy the lessening of stress that my training program provides me daily.

If you want to know more about the Masters Program, subscribe to *Swim Master* for $3.00 a year for six bimonthly issues. It is available by order from Mrs. June Krauser, 5340 N.E. 17th Avenue, Fort Lauderdale, Florida 33308. *Swim Master* lists scheduled Masters events, results of Masters events, meet information, rankings and records. There are also articles of specific interest to Masters swimmers.

GENERAL INFORMATION

In competitive swimming the two seasons, indoor and outdoor, are termed short and long course, respectively. The indoor season is conducted primarily in 25-yard and 25-meter pools. During the outdoor season meets may be conducted in pools of any of the following sizes: 25 yards, 25 meters, or 50 meters. Records and rankings are kept for both boys and girls at all levels of competition and for the various pool sizes—national, regional, and district. Within these divisions are records for Junior Olympic competition at national, regional, and district levels, which are kept separately, although a Junior Olympic record may or may not be the same as a record in a different competition.

The interscholastic and intercollegiate programs are completely separate and I will not try to describe them here. Suffice it to say they have their state, regional, and national championship events, records and rankings, plus a dual-meet season, all of which occurs during the academic year. Information about the scholastic and collegiate programs is obtainable from your high school athletic association and the National Collegiate Athletic Association (NCAA), whose address is U.S. Highway 50 and Nall Avenue, Shawnee Mission, Kansas 66222. The NCAA rule book may be ordered from the NCAA Publishing Service at the current price of $2.00.

In order to enter a meet, form a club, receive a sanction to hold a meet, or register an athlete, you must contact your district AAU association, whose address you can obtain from the National AAU headquarters in Indianapolis, Indiana. A swimmer may compete independent of a club as an "unattached" swimmer, as long as he conforms to regulations for AAU registration, but he may also wish to join a club and enjoy the group experience. He can obtain information about existing clubs or a schedule of meets from his district association, which will tell him whom to contact for entry blanks, etc.

This, very sketchily, will give you an idea of how amateur competitive swimming operates. It is only meant to acquaint you with the manner of its regulation in a very general way. I think it is enough to point you in the right direction, should you be interested.

There are a number of periodicals available on the subject of competitive swimming. Some are only statewide in scope. I won't try to list them since I would be sure to leave out a few. Two national publications exist in the United States: *Swimming World* and *Aquatic World*. *Aquatic World* (P.O. Box 366, Mountain View, California 94040, published bimonthly with a subscription cost of $3.50 per year) is relatively new and contains interviews and articles by professional writers. *Swimming World* (8622 Bellanca Avenue, Los Angeles, California 90045, published monthly with a yearly subscription cost of $9.00 to U.S. subscribers) has been in existence for over twenty years; it contains meet results, articles, a section for each of the aquatic programs (water polo, long-distance or marathon swimming, diving, synchronized swimming, and so on). Because it has been in existence for a long time, it has become the source of information for everything from rule changes to coaching vacancies; its advertisements give you information about everything from stopwatches to electronic timing devices. I mention these publications because people often write me asking for this information. They want to learn about the sport and I feel these publications provide the best way to do so.

Interest in swimming has grown greatly in the past few years and it is the Age-Group Program that is largely responsible. Most of our Olympic and national champions, such as Mark Spitz, have come up through the age-group ranks. In fact, it is getting harder all the time to find exceptions. There are presently hundreds of thousands of registered swimmers and they form the basis of our country's success at the Olympic level.

Coaches of swimming have formed several coaches' organizations, the two primary ones being the American Swim Coaches Association* and the College Swim Coaches Association. If you ever get to that point, you may want to join one of these organizations.

Last, but not least, we have an International Swimming Hall of Fame, located in Fort Lauderdale, Florida. I am proud to say that I am the founding president of the Hall of Fame. The executive director is William (Buck) Dawson. If you are ever in Fort Lauderdale, you might be interested in seeing the Hall's beautiful building, which is appropriately built on material dredged from the inland waterway and is located between a canal and the ocean. The Hall contains memorabilia of our sport's history, displays of current interest, and, of course, a pictorial record of each of the honorees who have been enshrined there.

*ASCA, Executive Director, Robert Ousley, International Swimming Hall of Fame, 1 Hall of Fame Drive, Fort Lauderdale, Florida.

Dr. James Counsilman is professor of physical education and swimming coach at Indiana University. He received his Ph.D. at the State University of Iowa and was the swimming coach of the Men's United States Olympic Team in 1964 and again in 1976.